The Ugly Truth
The Dark Side of Borderline Personality Disorder & The Emotional Mind

The Ugly Truth
The Dark Side of Borderline Personality Disorder & The Emotional Mind

The Ugly Truth
The Dark Side of Borderline Personality Disorder & The Emotional Mind

The Ugly Truth
The Dark Side of Borderline Personality Disorder
&
The Emotional Mind
A Crazy & Obsessed Series (Book 3)

The Ugly Truth
The Dark Side of Borderline Personality Disorder & The Emotional Mind

The Ugly Truth
The Dark Side of Borderline Personality Disorder & The Emotional Mind

The Ugly Truth
The Dark Side of Borderline Personality Disorder
&
The Emotional Mind
A Crazy & Obsessed Series (Book 3)

©2020

The Ugly Truth
The Dark Side of Borderline Personality Disorder & The Emotional Mind

All rights reserved. No part of this publication may be reproduced, distributed, or transmitted in any form or by any means, including photocopying, recording, or other electronic or mechanical methods, without the prior written permission of the publisher, except in the case of brief quotations embodied in critical reviews and certain other noncommercial uses permitted by copyright law.

The Ugly Truth
The Dark Side of Borderline Personality Disorder & The Emotional Mind

Table of Contents

My Borderline Struggle
13

Case Studies
21

The Borderline Personality
30

Psychological Entitlement
34

The Consequences
40

Comorbidity
54

Darkness Beyond
64

The Chaos
71

The Ugly Truth
The Dark Side of Borderline Personality Disorder & The Emotional Mind

Controlled by Emotions
79

Emotional Prisoners
84

Tortured by Silence
89

Normopathy
94

Incapable of Sympathy
99

Humans are Impulsive
103

Struggle to See Beyond
109

Objectively Impossible
113

Stuck Inside Mind
116

The Ugly Truth
The Dark Side of Borderline Personality Disorder & The Emotional Mind

The Ugly Truth
The Dark Side of Borderline Personality Disorder & The Emotional Mind

The Ugly Truth
The Dark Side of Borderline Personality Disorder & The Emotional Mind

The Ugly Truth
The Dark Side of Borderline Personality Disorder & The Emotional Mind

Part One

The Ugly Truth
The Dark Side of Borderline Personality Disorder & The Emotional Mind

The Ugly Truth
The Dark Side of Borderline Personality Disorder & The Emotional Mind

My Borderline Struggle

My Story

Six years ago, my psychiatrist preemptively diagnosed me with Borderline Personality Disorder on accounts of my "fluctuating moods," "manipulative lies," and "exaggerated stories." What the hell? Borderline Personality Disorder? What in the world does that even mean? A personality disorder? Me? Are you kidding?

The Ugly Truth
The Dark Side of Borderline Personality Disorder & The Emotional Mind

What a joke! There's no way I could have a personality disorder. Is that even a real diagnosis? Personalities are supposed to fluctuate. No one can possibly have a stable personality all the time in all circumstances. That's ludicrous! This unqualified psychiatrist, with a master's degree in nonsensical lies, has no idea what she's talking about. I went to her for my depression, something I believe was also an overstatement, and now she's pointing out another mental illness in me? I bet it's just an injudicious scheme to try to render more money out of my insurance company.

I'm supposed to be distinctive; a personality disorder is the most preposterous disorder I have ever heard of. All I wanted were some simple pills, medication to paralyze and subdue the emotions that occluded my mind and made me hate my every being. I was not expecting to walk away with a brand-new label beneath my belt.

What the fuck is a borderline personality anyway? I refused to believe my verdict. Addicted to attention? False suicidal threats to prevent perceived abandonment? Constructed manipulations to deceive those around me into getting what I want? Destructive life behaviors due to impulsive decisions that I either fail to remember or deny later? None of those criteria sounded like me. Those all seemed concocted and used as justifications to diagnose me as "mentally insane" and throw me into the statistical pool of mental health diagnoses.

However, I was erroneous. Boy, was I mistaken! Have you ever heard of the saying, "You begin to behave like your label even when you weren't your label to begin with, just because someone in a white coat tells you that

The Ugly Truth
The Dark Side of Borderline Personality Disorder & The Emotional Mind

you are?" That's how I felt with my personality disorder diagnosis.

The more I was labeled and called my diagnosis, the more I slowly began to adopt it as truth. The more I started looking into my past actions based on the fabricated stories of several psychotherapists and psychiatrists, the more I began to forcefully connect the pieces together and believe a diagnosis I didn't even think was real.

Thinking back, my past relationships had all ended with me, on my knees, crying for attention, both during and after, even with people I never even dated. Breakups and unrequited love left me flailing and broken, a fish out of the water desperately searching for reasons to make others stay against their wills even if it meant I was seen as a sociopath while doing so.

I also somehow began to fear being alone and abandoned by those who didn't even matter to me, pawning for the slightest of attention just for the sake of having some. The end of relationships left me chaotic and frantic to replace the feeling of anguish and discomfort with literally anything I could grasp onto.

I developed strong attachments to anyone who acted like a parent and/or caretaker, exuding care or compassion, and I never gave relationships a fair chance to play through without feeling like I needed to control all parts of them.

I fled across the world on a whim to get away from myself after an excruciating breakup, somehow believing that was a therapeutic idea, only to end up calling my ex-

The Ugly Truth
The Dark Side of Borderline Personality Disorder & The Emotional Mind

partner from an airport halfway across the world, bawling my eyes out about how much I missed him even when I hated the relationship while I was in it.

I bounced back and forth between multiple short-term partners while craving for long-term companions I was never able to keep hold of, petrified to let any of them leave despite not being interested nor ready for the panic of ending up alone with no one. I always tried to have the loudest bark, engineering excuses, stories, and lies to get people to pay attention to and love me.

My impulsive actions never stood a chance when entering the realm of logical thinking; the strong instinctual and intuitive desire to take and demand overpowered any inch of common sense or rationality I had every single time. I purposely demolished positive aspects of my life in attempts to create unnecessary drama when I felt the current drama were not enough or when I felt attention steering away from my personal aura.

The constant need to feel more than I already was and want more than I actually deserved drove me into a hole I found difficult to crawl out of. The more my "tried and true" methods of manipulating others worked, the more inclined I became to use them despite who I shattered along the way. My struggle with a personality disorder I convinced myself to believe was existent left me with a constant personal battle of suicidal ideations and a disparaging lifestyle.

As a child, my parents never truly cared for me. Don't get me wrong, they were always there physically in terms of picking me up from school or feeding me when I was

The Ugly Truth
The Dark Side of Borderline Personality Disorder & The Emotional Mind

hungry, but they never truly understood me the way children believe their parents should. Even when they were around and physically nearby, I was still left feeling alone, neglected, and forgotten. I know, cliché, right?

My needs were never met mentally as I found myself constantly craving for love and affection, getting myself into accidents and injuring myself intentionally just to get my parents to notice me. Sometimes, my devious schemes worked. Other times, I found myself feeling even more disregarded and fragmented.

Most parents don't really understand the mental needs that children require in order to develop a mindset that does not become psychotic. The minds of young children are extremely malleable and easily influenced, so when they train themselves to believe a certain "truth" caused by their parents or someone close to them, they hold onto that belief as truth their entire lives, despite whether that belief is maniacal or malevolent.

Most parents believe that as long as their children have food on the table and clothing on their backs, then they are set for life. They fail to take the time to realize that children need to be nurtured and cared for mentally, to be understood and given the attention they seek rather than having their love bought with materialistic trinkets, or else they will seek it out elsewhere, including in damaging places. So, I did.

I sought out the care and attentiveness my parents failed to give me in the comfort of strange and random men, bouncing back and forth between men who paid the slightest of attention to me while taking advantage of and

The Ugly Truth
The Dark Side of Borderline Personality Disorder & The Emotional Mind

disregarding those I was already with. I began to see power in being able to grab the attention of people, casting them aside when I no longer needed them. This was the pattern in the endless mind-fucked cycle I called "dating."

However, at the same time, when I entered new relationships, more long-term and "stable" relationships than senseless hookups, I entered them hard, diving into them head first without fully getting to know who I was with and driving myself toward insanity when they attempted to leave, even after I had instigated the battles that caused them to want to walk away.

I saw each and every relationship like a puppet, a game which I could navigate freely when I wanted it to go my way despite my true animosity or affection toward them, and I had to have the relationships go my way or else I would feel like I could not breathe, hyperventilating with anxiety until I did something deadly to crush it.

I quickly turned from being extremely amorous and pleasurable to being withdrawn and antisocial to being neurotic and obsessed, chasing after those I neglected and never loved just because I dreaded ending up alone.

Loneliness was my biggest enemy. The fear of being left alone with my own mind drove me to a point where I would rather turn others against their own beliefs and intuitions than deal with the demons swarming inside my own mind. I guess my self-esteem was so low that sitting still with my own thoughts turned me into my own worst nemesis.

The Ugly Truth
The Dark Side of Borderline Personality Disorder & The Emotional Mind

Imagine your worst moment as a child where other kids would constantly torment you, making you feel awful about yourself, and eventually causing you to take those taunts in as truths and accept every lie and every flaw they spewed to heart. That is what solitude felt like whenever I was by myself, a never-ending session of being bullied, enough to cause me to tear out my hair and scream into oblivion.

Every new relationship I entered made me feel as if my life was complete, with all my dreams coming true and everything I had ever wanted falling into place, ecstatic. However, because of this, on the flip side, every end of a relationship also made me feel suicidal as if my heart was going to explode if I did not do everything I possibly could to stop these massacres from happening. It wasn't until the end of relationship three and endless psychotherapy sessions did I realize that the problem weren't the relationships or any of the men; the problem was me.

I was my own source of the rage, disappointment, self-criticism, guilt, and depression that I constantly blamed my ex-partners for causing me, remaining in constant denial as I refused to take responsibility for any of my own self-destructive and Machiavellian behaviors.

Each potentially delusional end left me trapped in a black hole I desperately tried to crawl out of by engaging in toxic stalking and self-injurious behaviors, living a statistic. My deep sense of insecurity and trepidation of not being good enough for romance drove me to refuse to accept the truth in that others were capable of leaving me despite how hard I tried to prevent them from doing so.

The Ugly Truth
The Dark Side of Borderline Personality Disorder & The Emotional Mind

The feeling of being left behind made me feel unwanted, used, and unloved. The thought of being forgotten made me revert to my child-like states, begging and pleading for attention from these ex-partners as if they were my caretakers and my life depended on them, propelling me into a further state of melancholy and apprehension.

Case Studies

Fear of Abandonment

As an easily influenced young child with a malleable and developing brain, Rachel was often ignored and neglected by her parents and left alone in the house. She had multiple babysitters at a time to whom she became attached, physically and mentally, just to watch them all leave, one by one, leaving her in tears and confusion.

Her mother never held her, and her father never told her he loved her. As she grew up, she became increasingly

The Ugly Truth
The Dark Side of Borderline Personality Disorder & The Emotional Mind

afraid of developing attachments toward anyone or anything for the fear that they will all leave her too, recreating the traumatic experiences and moments she suffered as a child.

However, when she entered college, she became obsessed with her philosophy professor. He was rugged and handsome, and she was certain that he was the person who would finally stick around and want to be in a relationship with her based on his beliefs on loyalty and trust. She wanted him. She enticed him, but he refused.

She became anxious and concerned that he would abandon her too, something she refused to let happen even though they were never together in the first place. So, she pursued him, doing everything she could to keep him from walking out of her life. When he transferred her out of his class, she followed him to his home.

When he refused to return her calls after she looked up his phone number on the school directory, she told his wife they were having an affair even when they weren't. She became extremely jealous when she saw him kissing his wife, and she slashed her tires early one morning. Rachel refused to stop her avenging behaviors, even when he filed a restraining order against her and moved out of state.

She became so focused on this one man and so terrified of the heartache that came with abandonment that she continued to follow him over the next seven years as he moved from country to country in attempts to escape. Her motivation became delusional for pursuing a man who never returned the same feelings, and she finally overdosed on mixed medications out of despair and desolation one evening in her car outside his home and died.

Rachel was so hyper-focused on her one goal that she was unable to calm herself down from her disturbed thoughts and behaviors. Her overwhelming emotions prevented her from thinking logically, and as a result, she reacted in inappropriate ways in attempts to stop the constant ringing and chattering inside her head.

She knew she needed to stop her infatuated patterns of behavior, but the piercing inside her mind pushed her to keep going. Her harrowing memories and past horrors of abandonment caused her to create a false attachment and perceived desertion toward a man who was never hers in the first place.

She idolized a hallucination with this man and lost contact with reality, engaging in behaviors that harmed both herself and those around her, threatening to harm herself if he didn't return her love, and eventually taking her own life.

Impulsive Behavior and Sensation Seeking

Madison was a straight-A student in high school, always obeying the rules and behaving as she was told, pleasing those around her. However, during her first job after graduation, she felt a sense of "feeling out of place" and "unfulfillment." She felt like she didn't belong in her mundane job as a nurse and itched to find something she loved, something she swore would complete her life once she figured out what that was.

The Ugly Truth
The Dark Side of Borderline Personality Disorder & The Emotional Mind

She wanted the drive that made her feel more than the numbness she continued to experience. Decades of being mentally trapped under the rules of others made her feel out of touch with herself, and she no longer knew who she was or what she wanted. All she knew was she needed to experience some kind of thrill.

She impulsively quit her job, began shooting up on cocaine, drank heavily every night, and became a prostitute, all just to feel the "thrill" of being alive. She was intelligent but remained in constant denial of her actions, refusing to acknowledge the harm she was putting herself through. She knew her actions were out of control, but she refused to stop.

Soon, she became pregnant, not knowing who the father was, and she had an abortion without even thinking through the consequences of those her action was affecting. She continued to steal from her parents over the next ten years without ever feeling guilt or shame.

Madison became emotionless as she quickly watched her life flush down the drain. Every night, she sat in her bath tub and cut her arm to relieve the numbing pain she felt inside. She hated her life, and she felt as if she could never go back to the life that used to be.

The human brain possesses a "braking system" that prevents individuals from steering wildly out of control when decisions seem out of the ordinary, and to prevent the mind from shattering into impulsive thoughts and the body from crumbling into reckless behaviors when emotions go awry.

The Ugly Truth
The Dark Side of Borderline Personality Disorder & The Emotional Mind

People with Borderline Personality Disorder, however, possess braking systems that have become defective or malfunctioned in that they are no longer able to control the constant waves of emotions that devastate them, causing them to crash into a flood of consequences before their actions have been thought thoroughly through.

Madison was unable to control her powerful emotions and confused cravings of "what if" so she acted out with impulsive and self-destructive behaviors in attempts to curb her anxiety. She engaged in reckless behaviors with strangers and alienated herself from her body.

She jumped head first into promiscuous activities without thinking about sexual transmitted diseases or pregnancy until it was too late, and she experienced internal rage that eventually caused her to become suicidal.

Despite acknowledging that her behaviors were destructive, Madison refused to stop because her damaging behaviors also provided thrill and sensation, rushes of adrenaline and excitement when sexually acting out, binge eating, and abusing drugs that were strong enough to overcome all logic.

Unstable Relationships and Destructive Behaviors

Bridget started a seemingly healthy relationship with a man she "loved," spending day and night with her partner. However, six months in, Bridget began feeling bored in the romantic connection and started picking fights with her boyfriend out of nowhere. She told him white lies just to get him heated so his full focus would turn to her. She pretended she wanted to break up with him just to see him prove his love to her.

She started arguments from nothing and refused to back down until she won, even when she didn't stand by her own words. She only felt love toward her boyfriend when he was not around and when he was, she pretended like he didn't exist.

A year into their relationship, she noticed that her boyfriend was becoming detached. The feelings they had felt for each other the first day they met had disappeared, and she became excessively suspicious of his actions and intentions. She called him day and night to make sure he wasn't cheating on her. She showed up at his apartment in the middle of the night to tell him she loved him, and she became angry when he told her he preferred a few minutes where she wasn't smothering him nonstop.

His words made her become so afraid of him leaving that she became even more insecure. She grew livid toward and envious of every woman he spoke to even his mother and sister. She even threatened to kill herself whenever he chose to spend time alone instead of with her, continuing to suspect his adulterous behaviors even when he remained loyal to her.

Ultimately, he decided he could no longer handle her drama and overbearingness, and he broke up with her. As expected, this drove her insane. She needed to hold on even when he rejected her, buying him a ring and proposing to him at his place of work. She bombarded his phone with text messages, ranging from how much she missed and loved him to how much she wanted him dead.

The Ugly Truth
The Dark Side of Borderline Personality Disorder & The Emotional Mind

She stalked him endlessly, telling herself she was allowed to because he was "hers," and she could do what she wanted as a result.

One day, while he was walking to his car to go to work, she came out from behind the tree where she had been hiding for the past week and stabbed him in the chest, whispering, "I love you," as he fell, bleeding, to the ground.

Bridget had a black and white, dichotomous point of view. She went back and forth between believing her boyfriend was perfect and believing he was the devil. One minute, she was smothering him and the next, she wanted nothing to do with him.

Individuals with Borderline Personality Disorder, or BPD, have difficulty understanding the "grey" area, leaving them with the "go away / please don't go" state of mind, making it difficult for them to maintain stable relationships as they continue to instigate fights and create unnecessary drama to feel a sense of arousal, only resorting to "love" when the other person wants to leave.

BPD is typically mirrored through erratic moods, turbulent personal relationships, the inability to control anger, and self-destructive behaviors. People who suffer from Borderline Personality Disorder are frequently irate and quick to take offense at every word or action related or unrelated to them.

For causes not apparent to others, BPD victims unexpectedly become sad, irritable, nervous, or angered. They find trouble in accepting life as is without the constant need to stir up anger or drama. They fear abandonment, but at the same time, provoke it repeatedly by plaguing others with unreasonable complaints and demands. They either vilify or extol others and themselves, a condition known as "Splitting."

These sudden rejections are often followed by intense attachments or increased attention-seeking behaviors. In the mind of a BPD victim, one single person can be both a saint and the devil, roles that switch back and forth when this one person fails to meet impossible standards and expectations of the BPD victims.

Long-term ambitions and dependability often contradict a "borderliner's" personality where they lack a clear sense of self to remain a stable mindset without constantly seeking more, often talking about frustration and inner loneliness without grounds to hold their statements up on.

Borderliners engage in risky behaviors such as reckless driving, excessive spending, irresponsible drinking, and promiscuous sexual activity, as well as express threats of false suicidal ideations and desires, engage in attempted suicide without the desire for actual death, and execute self-mutilation as a means to grab the attention of others but only when others are around to witness their cries for help because they often tend to see the slightest of problems as catastrophic and unsolvable.

People with BPD experience emotional and unpredictable shifts of sensations, and they often find it difficult to maintain a steady ground after unleashing these emotions. The rapidly shifting emotional environment of

The Ugly Truth
The Dark Side of Borderline Personality Disorder & The Emotional Mind

people with BPD forces those around them to walk on eggshells, cautious of speaking or acting in ways that could further trigger the BPD victims.

People with BPD can also experience serenity, anger, depression, and euphoria all within a span of a few minutes, often causing people to mistaken them with victims of Bipolar Disorder, leaving Borderline Personality Disorder a misunderstood mental illness and phenomenon, often left unnoticed, untreated, and forgotten.

The Borderline Personality

What is Borderline Personality Disorder?

Borderline Personality Disorder is a psychological condition marked by persistent inconsistency or recurrent instability in emotions, mood, perceptions of the self and others, personal relationships, and self-esteem.

Approximately 10-14% of the general population and 15-20% of patients in psychiatric hospitals suffer from

The Ugly Truth
The Dark Side of Borderline Personality Disorder & The Emotional Mind

BPD, more often than not, as a comorbid disorder with another chronic mental illness. The prevalence of this disease for women is 2-3 times higher than for men, similar to how women often suffer more from depression than men.

This increased occurrence has often been linked to premenstrual anxiety, incestuous relationships, or harassments from close family members during childhood, conditions more widespread in women than in men.

This persistent or intermittent victimization and brutalization eventually leads to weakened relationships, foreseeable failure and pain, increased distrust in men, and an over-concern with sexuality, sexual promiscuity, lack of inhibitions, deep-seated depression, and a seriously damaged sense of self.

According to the American Psychiatric Association's Diagnostic and Statistical Manual of Mental Disorders (DSM-5), personality disorders are characterized as persistent, omnipresent, and inflexible patterns of vision, thought, and/or actions that cause severe disorder or deficiency in the minds of human beings. These behaviors include struggles in personal relationships, incoherent and irrational cognitive habits, and poor management of urges and emotions.

Individuals with personality disorders are often difficult to live and work with because they struggle with proper and appropriate reactions to stressors of anxiety and constructive criticisms.

The Ugly Truth
The Dark Side of Borderline Personality Disorder & The Emotional Mind

Borderline Personality Disorder (BPD) is a mental ailment that results in a twisted self-image, impulsive behaviors, unpredictable and intense relationships, and extreme emotional responses toward normal circumstances. People with BPD find it challenging to normalize their thoughts and mindsets, leading them to self-harming and self-demoting activities.

BPD is more commonly seen in western cultures and societies, where the concepts of "individualism" and "independence" are more widespread. Western societies measure and promote the value of success based on how much individuals achieve in both their professional and social lives in COMPARISON to those around them, pressuring individuals to live a constant life of competition or risk "falling out" and "losing."

This idealism makes people strive to create drastic differences between them and their peers, stepping away from the commonalities and norms of traditional society to achieve greater goals beyond the scope of ordinary life. Because of this lifestyle, most westerners develop a phenomenon known as "Self-Absorption," which have been highly correlated with BPD.

Self-absorption drives individuals to focus on a single aspect of life, aka themselves, and as a result, they develop this increased desire to improve the self through any means possible, including risking the emotional health of both themselves and others by constantly seeking attention through radical measures even when that self-absorbed attention is not validated.

The Ugly Truth
The Dark Side of Borderline Personality Disorder & The Emotional Mind

Eastern societies, on the other hand, function more as social groups rather than as individuals. They prioritize giving and sharing rather than taking, adopting a more selfless belief in attempts to promote the greater good of society and others rather than themselves.

Because of this, easterners are less likely to fall into the temptation of developing the "Me Syndrome," where the focus of everyone else needs to be on them. There is less of a drive to engage in intense and impulsive behaviors to thwart attention toward the self.

Psychological Entitlement

What is Psychological Entitlement?

The term "Psychological Entitlement" refers to the belief that specific individuals or groups of individuals are entitled to earn more or deserve more than others without reason. They focus on the ideas of "right," "deservingness," and believe that when people contribute to a cause or to a situation, they are obligated to receive something in return for their contributions, a term known as "Psychological Privilege."

However, as we all know, this is usually not the case when it comes to the game of life, and so when people do not receive what they believe they are entitled to, they become extremely upset, viewing the situation(s) as "unjust" or "unfair," seeking out compensation for their work even if they do not deserve it and refusing to contribute further to causes even when their contributions were minor.

Psychological privilege creates individual differences between those with extremely high psychological entitlement levels and those with moderate to low psychological entitlement levels.

Those with high levels of psychological privilege are more inclined to believe they are more deserving than others are even when they are not, while those with low levels of psychological privilege fail to believe they are deserving even when they actually are and constantly pull their levels of self-esteem down.

Individuals with high levels psychological entitlement are more likely to agree with statements involving "wanting more," "being liked," and "deserving better" on the self-report Psychological Entitlement Scale because their minds have been construed into them believing they deserve more, a phenomenon where they truly believe they are worthy rather than just pretending they are worthy due to self-absorbed opinions of themselves or egotistical thoughts.

The Ugly Truth
The Dark Side of Borderline Personality Disorder & The Emotional Mind

When psychological entitlement is represented in romantic relationships, there is an increased havoc of negative consequences on relational behavior, thoughts, and emotions. Individuals in relationships who report having high levels of psychological entitlement often respond negatively to relational conflicts and are often less empathetic, less respectful, and less willing to understand the perspectives of their romantic partners.

These individuals are also the ones who are more prone to aggressive behaviors, feelings of rage, and are more likely to act violent toward their partners, especially those who criticize them or challenge their opinions, a positive correlation with domestic abuse and assault.

BPD victims who struggle to accept the negative consequences of life and relationships are more likely to become increasingly susceptible to overwhelming emotional distress and distraught. Individuals with high levels of psychological superiority often expect experiencing positive feelings and outcomes as fundamental human rights, becoming agitated and disappointed when the universe fails to align with their needs. As a result, they resort to brute force and manipulation to re-rotate the universe until it does meet their desires and expectations.

Hallmarks of healthy personalities and mindsets include the ability to tolerate frustration and delayed gratification, and a resilience to intense adversities in life even when they seem unfair rather than falling through the cracks of the obstacles that come with the complexities of life.

The Ugly Truth
The Dark Side of Borderline Personality Disorder & The Emotional Mind

Interpersonal symptoms that often co-occur with borderline personality individuals include physical, sexual, and mental abuse, both in childhood and adulthood. These patterns of abuse trigger a chain-reaction of increased inappropriate efforts to avoid abandonment, impulsive suicidal and self-harm behaviors, and chaotic personal relationships due to a desperation to avoid abandonment distress.

Childhood abuse makes it difficult for adults later on in life to feel secure about their relationships with other people as children are often vulnerable to initial impressions. They develop the negative impressions they have experienced into core beliefs, such as, "I'll never be good enough for love," "I will always be alone forever," "No one cares about me because my life is useless and insignificant," and "If they won't stay, I'll have to make them stay," causing them to lack faith in those they are supposed to trust, such as parents and caregivers, and force trust from others instead.

Psychological trauma manifests in emotional damage as a result of distressing incidents, where those individuals affected lose their abilities to cope with the overwhelming stress that encompasses them. These distressing incidents can either be perceived as hallucinated threats or actual threats of physical and/or psychological harm.

BPD victims commonly experience psychological distress from past or existing traumatic memories, or they subconsciously create pre-constructed thoughts of past or existing traumatic memories that never existed.

The Ugly Truth
The Dark Side of Borderline Personality Disorder & The Emotional Mind

Traumatic events or incidents that result in borderline personality behaviors and judgments are extremely subjective. What is perceived as disturbing versus what is not solely depends on the person experiencing the defining moment.

The definition of "traumatic" depends on how the affected individual defines it, assigns value to it, and is physically and psychologically disturbed by the situation. A situation that is seen as "traumatic" is most often an occurrence that correlates with a sense of embarrassment or disappointment, causing the individual to become silenced, rather than an incident that causes physical or mental pain.

In many cases, embarrassment and shame are the largest factors associated with trauma. It is much easier to become psychologically scarred by moments that demean the self-esteem and pride than by moments that cause physical or mental pain such as sexual abuse or harassment.

Other factors that contribute to how a particular individual defines trauma include cultural and societal beliefs, the availability of surrounding social support, and the developmental stage of the individual's mental state.

Borderline Personality Disorder drastically takes a toll on its victims' self-perceptions of themselves and their surrounding situations, causing them to react in ways that are generally not part of the norm nor accepted by society. Their intense fears of losing attention or those they claim to love drive them toward a mental state where they partake in extreme measures to prevent this actual

The Ugly Truth
The Dark Side of Borderline Personality Disorder & The Emotional Mind

or imagined perception of abandonment, leading to dysfunctional relationships.

The paranoia caused by their assumptions and premonitions causes their personalities to switch within the blink of an eye as they transition from seemingly loving in relationships to revengeful and loathing without reason or trigger. They experience extreme mood swings that are both unexpected to themselves and others, lasting from a few hours to a few days.

This phenomenon is known as "Emptiness Feelings," where individuals lose contact with reality and engage in risky behaviors that are detrimental to their well-beings, constantly seeking something that does not exist and throwing aside their stable careers, relational connections, and values to chase after uncertainty.

The Consequences

Physiological and Psychological Consequences

Victims of Borderline Personality Disorder can experience extreme and intermittent panic attacks, especially when their means of seeking attention and preventing abandonment have failed, causing them to feel near death unless they achieve their goals of manipulation.

Panic attacks are manifested by waves of fear driven by an abrupt and immobilizing force, causing the victims to feel as if their lifespans are shortening. Sufferers report

The Ugly Truth
The Dark Side of Borderline Personality Disorder & The Emotional Mind

feeling increased tension and anxiety paired with shortness of breath and the feeling of their hearts uncontrollably beating out of their chests.

However, panic attacks are usually triggered in those with BPD, coming and going as different situations arise, such as the reoccurrence of romantic relationship separations with the same or different people or other panic-inducing situations where individuals feel threatened and unable to escape their own apprehensive mentalities.

Shame often goes hand-in-hand with attention-seeking behaviors in victims of BPD, frantically trying to prevent themselves from experiencing humiliation and mortification so much so to the point where they do whatever they can to manipulation situations to avoid the shame.

Shame is a conscious emotion that constantly reminds us of self-inadequacy, indignity, dishonor, remorse, and disconnection, a sign that specific situations or people have disturbed our positive feelings and optimistic mindsets. Constant and repetitive shocks of shame cause individuals to perceive themselves as flawed, damaged, and deranged, unable to fit in with the rest of the world so they seek out drastic measures to save themselves from being seen as "imperfect."

Desperate motives to avoid experiencing shameful feelings can often lead to addiction as BPD victims anxiously strive for admiration and responsiveness from those who threaten them by engaging in radical actions that prevent what is deservingly theirs from being taken

The Ugly Truth
The Dark Side of Borderline Personality Disorder & The Emotional Mind

away. They tend to correlate success with attention and believe that unless they are likeable and favored by all, then their lives and reputations are meaningless and worth nothing.

The terms "anger" and "rage" are often misunderstood by many as interchangeable. Although anger and rage are both considered results of emotional outbursts, they are correlated rather than mutually exclusive, as anger is simply a fleeting and temporary feeling that a person experiences when he or she feels offended or betrayed, while rage is an action of revenge and retaliation, a consequence that arises from the feeling of anger.

Rage is an intense expression of wrath and hatred that results when an individual is unable to properly control his or her anger. Anger, on the other hand, is often perceived as a healthy and normal means of expressing the self, an emotion that can usually be controlled or quelled if tackled from the right direction.

Rage is often perceived as a toxin that plagues and destroys the human mind, driving it toward a state of self-destruction when the lives of others and situations around them do not align with their own, making them unable to cease until the mind has been demolished to the point of no return.

Rage can sometimes manifest as a complete blackout of consciousness, where individuals cannot recall their actions when they were in the state of rage, their bodies behaving in ways that were disconnected from their minds.

The Ugly Truth
The Dark Side of Borderline Personality Disorder & The Emotional Mind

Borderliners often experience rage when they behave in unpredictable ways; their anger motivating them to seek and do all they can to achieve their irrational and illogical goals, turning into weapons of self-destruction when they realize life continues to move on regardless of whether they achieve what they desire.

The dichotomous mindset of borderliners also makes it difficult for them to recognize feelings as transient emotions that can be disregarded rather than as strong forces that overpower their entire bodies and cause them to pursue and attain despite their deadly methods.

Many victims of BPD often express feeling "hollow" or "empty" on the inside, like there is a hole deep inside them aching to be filled but unsure of what is needed to fill it. Because of this, they constantly crave for something, something more that they are not able to identify or obtain, leaving them feeling lonely and unfulfilled, mindlessly trying to fill that void with shallow activities such as sex, drugs, and/or food.

However, because of this inability to identify their true source of emptiness, these shallow replacements are often never enough to truly satisfy their cravings, simply feeding into a dark, black hole instead. The more they attempt to fill this never-ending hole of emptiness, the more they fuel their impulsivity as they resort to jumping into decisions and actions without thinking through the dangerous penalties of their risky judgments.

Famous philosopher, Baruch Spinoza, once described sadness as "transferring a person from great perfection to smaller perfection." Sadness or sorrow is a mood that resembles an increased sense of disadvantage, failure, loss, and dejection.

When this emotion persists for extended periods of time, chronic depression and suicidal thoughts often result, leaving the ones affected feeling silenced, crestfallen, and withdrawn into the self, lacking the desire to engage in interests that were once appealing.

When these lingering feelings of melancholy are paired with severe and transient mood swings, they begin to resemble symptoms of Borderline Personality Disorder, an illness often confused with Bipolar Disorder.

However, the key difference between those with Bipolar Disorder and those who suffer from Borderline Personality Disorder is that victims of BPD more often than not act out because they have motives of seeking attention and believe their conducts of abnormal actions will help them achieve their sensational goals.

Paranoid and dichotomous ways of thinking that are seen as abnormal to the average human being become standard ways of behavior for those with BPD, including disturbing and demotivating thoughts on how they are terrible people for existing or how their lives do not matter as much as others.

These thoughts lead to uncertainties about their sense of selves as they experience extreme lows and paralysis for terse, but repetitive, periods of time. This paranoia results in constant anxiety over thoughts of loved ones leaving or abandoning them, the fears of separation causing them to act out in attached, dependent, and envious manners,

The Ugly Truth
The Dark Side of Borderline Personality Disorder & The Emotional Mind

often accusing their romantic partners of actions not being committed just to develop that sense of security.

When accusations and confrontations fail to resolve their worries, borderliners resort to obsessive stalking behaviors, accusing those around them of infidelity and tracking the steps of those who stay and leave. This paranoia can become so intense that BPD victims often find it difficult to separate reality from their constructed false accusations, believing and experiencing past "memories" of events that never existed in the first place.

This leads to patterns of dysfunctional relationships where those suffering find themselves extremely attached one minute with intense loathing toward the same partners the next minute, or becoming bored of those they are with only after a couple months and seeking out attention from others due to the initial thrill of being wanted and loved, constantly placing threats on their current relationships.

BPD victims often experience two types of behavioral impulses: a self-harming impulse and a self-destructive impulse. Self-harming impulses often include physical injuries to the selves, such as individuals cutting their arms with razor blades or purposely burning themselves on hot surfaces to feel any sensation. These impulses are usually driven by feelings of numbness or sadness, causing them to harm themselves in order to feel or as cries for help for unwarranted attention.

Self-destructive impulses, on the other hand, are portrayed in the form of reckless and irresponsible behaviors such as binge drinking, toxic drug abuse, excessive promiscuity, overeating, aggressive driving, shoplifting, destruction of property (self or others), and spending or gambling even when they are in extreme debt.

These sorts of impulses drive people to jump into risks before thinking through the consequences of those risks, such as the dangers involved in unprotected sexual behaviors, the deaths that could result from excessive drug use, and potential criminal records that could result from acts of kleptomania.

Self-destructive impulses are also often paired with fits of severe rage when these compulsions are halted or stalled from fruition, such as getting caught when trying to steal a magazine that was potentially seen as "the thing" to fill the emptiness inside or becoming bankrupt because playing that round of cards was the "satisfaction" needed for fulfillment, driving borderliners to seek out other, sometimes deadlier, ways to justify their needs.

Borderliners often claim to desire stable and healthy relationships, but time after time, they unintentionally hinder and destroy their chances of maintaining positive relationships. They have constant worries about failing to meet relationship expectations and maintaining positive relationships that they subconsciously seek out flaws in their partners and relationships even when there are none.

These insecurities tend to amplify when relationships become more developed and stable as borderliners repeatedly tell themselves they do not deserve love or happiness, that something must be wrong for their partners to stay, and they continue to question whether

The Ugly Truth
The Dark Side of Borderline Personality Disorder & The Emotional Mind

they are making mistakes until the stable relationships eventually do come to an end.

When these relationships end, borderliners are driven into the arms of those offering unstable relationships, those who confirm their self-destructive thoughts and anxieties, leaving them even more broken and prone to increase their borderline thoughts of wanting more and more attention from more and more toxic people.

The intense desires of those with BPD for relationships and "love" are often driven by overwhelming needs to fill the endless void inside their hearts.

However, borderliners struggle to maintain these relationships as they wrestle back and forth between making both their disease and their partners happy, a constant push and pull as both sides battle it out in the borderliner's mind, eventually coming to a crash and spiraling into a cycle of disappointment, delusion, and anger when the borderliner is unable to satisfy the needs of either side.

Partners of borderliners often find it challenging to maintain steady relationships with them as they find it difficult to satisfy their constant desires for attention and their unconventional lives of impulsivity.

But, beware, borderliners are difficult to spot, and those who enter romantic relationships with them do not realize what they are capable of until it becomes too late. Borderliners tend to begin relationships with high hopes and enthusiasm, seeming like the "perfect partner."

The Ugly Truth
The Dark Side of Borderline Personality Disorder & The Emotional Mind

They provide comfort, compassion, and excitement, making their partners feel loved and wanted like most partners in normal, stable relationships. However, these acts of love, respect, and passion are all short-lived as the positive optimism of borderliners can quickly turn into negative responses and aloofness.

It does not take long into entering a new relationship before borderliners are triggered into suspiciousness and life-threatening anxiety, leading them to revert to dependent and clingy child-like states where they feel physically and mentally unable to let their partners go for the fear of being left alone again like they once were by their caretakers.

As a result of this foreseeable potential neglect, they engage in overly insecure behaviors such as excessively calling their partners (even in the middle of the night), physically sticking to the sides of their partners at all hours of the day (even when their partners are at their places of work), and becoming angry and skeptical when their partners ask for even a few minutes of space.

Victims of BPD commonly associate "asking for space" with infidelity and rejection, unable to see that people are naturally independent and have minds and lives of their own; entering into relationships do not mean the partners need to stick by each other's sides at all times, a truth unbeknownst to most borderliners.

Rather than acknowledging reality and the norms of life, borderliners become irrationally angry when their partners request time away from them, threatening to harm themselves if their partners do not physically stay

The Ugly Truth
The Dark Side of Borderline Personality Disorder & The Emotional Mind

with them at all times, and becoming jealous and seeking revenge when partners do decide to walk out, whether temporarily or permanently, sometimes even threatening to harm the partners' family members and friends, whom borderliners view as the nemeses who try to take their partners away from them.

Borderliners in relationships also teeter back and forth between feeling breathless and taken away by love, loving their partners until death, and feeling distant and emotionally withdrawn toward their partners, loathing them and not wanting anything to do with them, constantly lashing out with verbal abuse and denial toward their partners until they reach their breaking points and hint toward separation. That is when the gears inside the borderliners' minds switch.

Similar to their views toward themselves and life in general, individuals with BPD also possess a dichotomous perception when it comes to romance, portraying a "love-hate" relationship with themselves and with their partners.

Unlike "normal" individuals who enter relationships, borderliners either see their relationships as "perfect" or "destined for disaster." One small argument or one slight disagreement is enough to automatically trigger borderliners to assume their relationships are coming to an end, unable to compromise or live in the "grey areas" of how seemingly "normal" relationships are supposed to function.

An individual with Borderline Personality Disorder often experiences a demoralized or uncertain sense of self,

The Ugly Truth
The Dark Side of Borderline Personality Disorder & The Emotional Mind

feeling inadequate or fundamentally flawed with no apparent reason, along with constant switches in how they feel about themselves and how this feeling affects their relations with those around them.

Their seemingly inexplicable anger, impulsiveness, and mood swings often push others away despite the intense desires of the borderliners to experience loving relationships. This rapid switch in personalities and the manners in which they understand themselves is known as "Identity Diffusion," where the individuals actively change their perceptions about themselves, feeling "on top of the world" one minute to "nonexistent" the next.

This unstable image of the self leads to eventual existential crisis and frequent changes in jobs, friendships, relationship partners, aspirations, and beliefs. The crisis of the unknown is one of the most common causes of self-injuring and risk-taking behaviors.

The constant shift in personality and goals of an individual suffering from BPD can cause their partners to become confused as to who they fell in love with, leading to relationship turmoil when the BPD victim cycles between love and hate.

One key characteristic of a borderliner is interpersonal hypersensitivity, meaning they find difficulty in maintaining stable and mutual beneficial relationships with others, always taking offense from what others say and never being able to truly trust the words of someone else. Romantic BPD relationships are often painful and conflict-laden, starting fights when nothing is wrong and become apprehensive that the partners will leave even when there are no signs that point to it.

On the other hand, they can also quickly shift to feeling smothered and afraid of intimacy with no apparent triggers, withdrawing from their partners just as quickly as they attach to them. The resulting consequence of these shifts is an inexorable back and forth pull between affection and attention to abrupt detachment and loneliness.

Borderliners also experience a phenomenon known as "Vulnerability to Abandonment," a condition where they constantly watch for signs of people who will leave them or people who will consider leaving them, even if these signs are minor such as a night out with their friends without the borderliners or a small family trip without external parties, and borderliners perceive these minor events as premonitions of separation and abandonment.

These "signs" drive borderliners to engage in extreme measures to prevent their premonitions from becoming reality, including public scenes of begging, stalking behaviors of their partners' every move, physically withholding their partners from walking out of their sights, and expressing dark lies, manipulating their partners by misrepresenting the truth and construing stories that provide leverage to prevent their partners from leaving such as feigning deadly illnesses like cancer or imminent responsibilities like pregnancy.

Although quarrels are often common and normal in healthy relationships, even the most minor of arguments, such as a partner mentioning to a borderline victim their

The Ugly Truth
The Dark Side of Borderline Personality Disorder & The Emotional Mind

dissatisfaction with how they failed to wash the dishes, can trigger an emotional downward spiral, causing the partners to feel like they are walking on eggshells.

Partners in BPD relationships are left feeling stuck and silenced, unable to discuss important issues or their own emotional feelings in the relationships without triggering a major conflict or having the borderliners threaten to harm themselves.

Borderliners often take the opinions and feelings of others personally, correlating the dissatisfactions of others toward an external situation with dissatisfactions toward the borderliners. They become defensive as they feel they are being attacked, and their minds instantly turn toward impending breakups and divorces when their partners are simply expressing their opinions and feelings.

When borderliners first enter relationships, they experience a phase known as "Idealization," where they place their partners on pedestals and feel like they are living in the "honeymoon phase." They falsely believe they have found their "perfect match," their soul mate who will save them eternal emotional pain and damnation…in every single new relationship they enter.

However, as the relationships progress, this idealization begins to diminish, reality sets in, and problems start to emerge, even if from nothing. When borderliners realize that their new partners are not faultless (this reality often sets in shortly after the relationships begin but can also occur years down the line), their idealized perfect images of their thought-to-be "soul mates" crash.

The Ugly Truth
The Dark Side of Borderline Personality Disorder & The Emotional Mind

Because borderliners often suffer from dichotomous thinking, they have extreme difficulties accepting flaws as part of human life and that everyone, even them, makes mistakes. As a consequence of this, their idealizations quickly turn to devaluations, and they begin perceiving their partners as horrible people, leading their partners to feel unloved and depreciated, and the cycle resumes.

Comorbidity

Borderline Personality Disorder Comorbidities

Psychiatric comorbidity is commonly found in most mental disorders, characterized as having the presence of two or more disorders in the same person at the same time, with symptoms of two separate diagnoses often overlapping and creating false diagnoses and a challenge in clinical treatment.

One of the most common comorbid symptoms that often coincides with Borderline Personality Disorder is an

The Ugly Truth
The Dark Side of Borderline Personality Disorder & The Emotional Mind

excessive need to harm the self, the physical body and mind included. Self-injurious behaviors are actions in which people engage in deliberate damage, such as self-harm or self-mutilation, toward their own bodies.

Self-harm behaviors usually occur when individuals want to inflict pain onto themselves as cries for help or as suicidal ideations, often leaving scars on their bodies as signs of psychological turmoil and causing damage to their tissues and veins to the point of no return. These are the individuals who usually want to die.

Self-mutilation, on the other hand, entails purposeful destruction or alteration of the body, such as extreme scarification, without the desire to actually harm the self to the point of death. However, this is not to say that people who self-mutilate do not also have suicidal thoughts, as many who self-mutilate also engage in suicide attempts that result in death from their injuries.

There is a common misconception that those who engage in self-harm or self-mutilation behaviors do so for attention as many also engage in these behaviors in the privacy of their own homes and make attempts to conceal their scars and wounds. The inflicted individuals can often become ashamed of these actions and hold them secret, especially if they are vulnerable and sensitive to rejection from others.

Self-injurious behaviors are common among individuals with Borderline Personality Disorder. Statistics show that over 40% of university students had engaged in self-harm or self-mutilation behaviors at least once while at least 10% had engaged in these behaviors at least ten times, with those who had experienced childhood abuse and neglect at higher risks.

Triggered by deep senses of desperation, uncontrolled depression, and a longing for death, suicidal behaviors tend to be more episodic and intermittent for borderliners as they often fluctuate between feeling fine and feeling despair, one of the most problematic aspects of BPD.

According to the World Health Organization (WHO), depression is the number one cause of illness worldwide, with over 300 million people suffering from this condition, with occurrences ranging from Major Depressive Disorder to Dysthymia to Postpartum Depression to Seasonal Affective Disorder.

Research has shown that almost 83% of individuals who suffer from Borderline Personality Disorder also suffer from a comorbid depressive condition. Because of this, many borderliners go unnoticed and are mistakenly diagnosed with a depressive disorder rather than a personality disorder.

Borderliners who experience comorbidity with depression often report feeling hostile and detached from other human beings, reporting passive-aggressive violence paired with active suicidal threats and co-occurring, non-lethal, self-injury behaviors.

They become dysfunctional, with extreme episodic dysphoria, recurrent temperament outbursts and agitation, depressive and anxious irritabilities, and feelings of loneliness and stress-related angst with serious dissociations.

The Ugly Truth
The Dark Side of Borderline Personality Disorder & The Emotional Mind

However, these depressive symptoms only arise in those suffering from BPD when they are triggered by an external force such as perceived rejection or abandonment, and they usually subside when these forces are eliminated as depressive symptoms are often forms of communication for how the individuals mentally feel.

But depressive symptoms in those with BPD are not always reported as simple sadness; BPD depressive symptoms have also been associated with feelings of anger, shame, loneliness, and emptiness, where borderliners report feeling jaded and agitated with desperate solitude when they are despondent, their depressive episodes often caused by interpersonal losses such as the loss of a relationship.

Depressive symptoms also include recurrent depressed and empty emotions, as well as feelings of guilt, worthlessness, and helplessness with a loss of interest in previously-enjoyed hobbies. Those suffering from depression also experience decreased strength, difficulty in focus, memory, and decision-making, and increased risks of drug, sex, and alcohol addictions, further complicating proper diagnosis of the personality disorder.

When addictions are paired with Borderline Personality Disorder, the BPD symptoms only amplify, increasing the antisocial and manipulative nature of these individuals. Addicts are just as likely, if not more likely, than borderliners to react impulsively and destructively, with mood swings ranging from severe depression to intense psychosis, and engage in acts of deceit and risky behaviors, further paralyzing and destabilizing their relationships, finances, and employment.

The Ugly Truth
The Dark Side of Borderline Personality Disorder & The Emotional Mind

Post-traumatic stress disorder, or PTSD, is a mental illness often caused by severely stressful situations, with major symptoms including hallucinations, nightmares, anxiety, and uncontrollable traumatic flashbacks, usually categorized into four classifications: disturbed thoughts, avoidance, negative thoughts, and mood changes. Many individuals who suffer from PTSD struggle with re-adapting to normal life and experience frequent reoccurrences of these symptoms periodically.

The comorbidity of BPD victims who also suffer from PTSD is between 25-60%, with sufferers of both types reporting early childhood trauma as opposed to those who only suffer from PTSD alone.

Individuals diagnosed with both BPD and PTSD generally experience more psychological and physical difficulties getting through life compared to those suffering from either BPD or PTSD, with increased complications in controlling their emotions and augmented mood swings and anger as a result of abandonment. This comorbidity also further increases the original symptoms of BPD, including emotional dysregulation, dissociation, attempted suicide, and self-mutilation.

Attention-deficit / hyperactivity disorder, or ADHD, is a chronic disorder that affects millions of young children and often persists into adulthood, affecting males at a higher prevalence than females as symptoms are more passive in females, with males becoming more hyperactive while females becoming less attentive.

Symptoms of ADHD include chronic difficulties in sustaining attention, hyperactivity, and persistent

The Ugly Truth
The Dark Side of Borderline Personality Disorder & The Emotional Mind

patterns of impulsive behavior that affect home, school, and work life. Symptoms often begin before the age of 12, with initial symptoms of low self-esteem and instability in interpersonal relationships for children.

Adults who struggle with ADHD, although not as common, find difficulty managing time, planning and setting goals, holding down a job, and often struggle with relationship issues, self-esteem, and increased addiction.

Literature consistently reports a high prevalence of co-occurring ADHD and BPD. Approximately 27% of an outpatient cohort of 372 individuals suffering from ADHD report also meeting BPD criteria based on the structured clinical interview for DSM-IV (SCID-II).

In another study of 181 adults, approximately 38% of individuals diagnosed with ADHD also met the criteria for Borderline Personality Disorder. A high co-occurrence rate was reported in a study of 118 adult females from outpatient clinics seeking treatment for BPD, where over 41% of these individuals met the criteria for ADHD during childhood and over 16% reported ADHD symptoms.

In a population survey by the National Epidemiological Survey on Alcohol and Related Conditions of more than 34,000 adults, they found that the lifetime comorbidity of BPD and ADHD is 33% while the prevalence of BPD alone in the general public is only 5.2%.

Impulsivity is a common overlap between those struggling from BPD and ADHD other than the two being considered "developmental" disorders with initial occurrences in childhood and adolescence.

However, despite the overlap in symptom, impulsivity in the sense of ADHD and impulsivity in the sense of BPD are drastically different. Impulsivity in ADHD includes constant interruptions and intrusions, often sticking their noses into the conversations of others even when unwarranted, and finding difficulty in remaining patient.

These behaviors in childhood can give rise to impairment of social functioning and self-damaging behaviors in adulthood, resulting in reckless driving, promiscuity, and aggression in interpersonal relationships, indirect results of childhood impulsivity.

Impulsivity in BPD victims, on the other hand, is characterized by direct self-damaging habits of reckless driving, promiscuity, and aggression in interpersonal relationships rather than acting as second-hand symptoms of another cause.

Eating disorders are another common comorbidity that is often found in individuals with BPD. Eating disorders are a series of psychological conditions that lead to unhealthy eating and exercise habits which can cause deadly health complications if left untreated.

Approximately 20 million women and 10 million men in the United States alone have or have had an eating disorder at some point in their lives, and by the age of 20, nearly 13% of Americans experience at least one type of eating disorder, with symptoms ranging from food

The Ugly Truth
The Dark Side of Borderline Personality Disorder & The Emotional Mind

restriction to food binging to purging behaviors such as vomiting and/or over-exercising.

Among all eating disorders, three of the most common types include Anorexia Nervosa, characterized by an obsessive fear of weight gain and an unrealistic perception of body image where sufferers see themselves as overweight even when they're not, Bulimia Nervosa, characterized by excessive use of purging behaviors such as vomiting, over-exercising, and/or laxatives and diuretics use in attempts to keep weight down and is often paired with impulsive behaviors, secrecy, and intense feelings of shame, guilt, and a lack of control, and Binge Eating Disorder, characterized by an uncontrollable need to eat, but unlike Bulimia Nervosa, is not paired with the compensatory need to dispel the food intake.

However, of all the major eating disorders, Bulimia Nervosa is the most prevalent as a comorbid disorder with BPD, with common overlapping symptoms including impulsive and out-of-control decision-making and a dichotomous thinking where bulimics feel a strong need to dispose of the food they consume or all hell breaks loose.

The purging desires of bulimics can become so strong that the individual deep within the wraths of the eating disorder are often strongly influenced by complicated feelings that overpower logic and reason, and the affected use their behaviors as methods of communication instead of words.

Although the exact relation between Bulimia Nervosa and Borderline Personality Disorder is not well known, eating disorder symptoms, such as purging, often begin as a coping mechanism for individuals, providing temporary relief and numbness for the intense feelings of depression and anxiety being experienced, leading the individuals to continuously return to these symptoms for further relief.

Furthermore, sufferers may also engage in self-harm behaviors as a means of punishing themselves for the guilt and shame they feel from their purging behaviors. According to a study by Dr. Mary Zanarini and her colleagues at McLean Hospital, individuals suffering from Borderline Personality Disorder have a higher chance of also developing eating disorders than the general population without this condition.

She revealed that over 53% of patients with BPD also met the criteria for at least one other eating disorder, 21.7% for Anorexia Nervosa and 24.1% for Bulimia Nervosa, compared to the 24.6% prevalence rate for all other personality disorders. Bulimia Nervosa individuals are predicted to have a higher comorbidity rate with BPD because victims of both illnesses have connections with physical, emotional, and sexual trauma during their childhoods, placing them at higher risks.

Roughly 80% of individuals with Borderline Personality Disorder experience some sort of suicidal behavior, including self-cutting, self-burning, and literal suicidal attempts. This is because they often experience this impulsivity of "having to" commit suicide when they don't get their ways, living mindsets of live-or-die situations.

The Ugly Truth
The Dark Side of Borderline Personality Disorder & The Emotional Mind

Because of this impulsivity, individuals with BPD are more likely to commit suicide than any other psychiatric disorder, with 4-9% of individuals with BPD who will die by suicide, 50 times higher than the suicide rate of the general population.

This increased rate is likely due to painful negative emotions that sufferers often try to quell with further actions, with the most common ways being through self-injury and substance abuse. These suicidal ideations can have lasting effects on individuals with BPD, leading them to reject potentially beneficial treatment methods.

According to brain imaging scans, individuals with BPD have increased abnormalities in the metabolism and structure of their brains when compared to healthy individuals, which explains why they tend to have increased impulsiveness and aggression.

Research has shown that there is less grey matter in individuals who are more prone to high suicide lethality while those with low suicidal lethality have increased grey matter in their brains.

Of the BPD victims who had attempted suicide, roughly 89% of individuals were shown to have less grey matter than their counterparts, and out of the BPD victims who had not attempted suicide, only 56% of these individuals had decreased grey matter, showing that decreased grey matter in the brain has a positive correlation with successful suicide behaviors and BPD symptoms.

Darkness Beyond

Darkness Beyond BPD

Internal control and the dysregulation of self-esteem are closely related to the false perception of grandeur that results from feelings of inferiority, fear, and worthlessness in which individuals feel the need to compensate for their low self-esteem with an increased sense of superiority, exceptionally high self-centeredness, delusions of unfulfilled desires, and limitless achievement, creativity, and elegance.

The Ugly Truth
The Dark Side of Borderline Personality Disorder & The Emotional Mind

However, grandiosity is malleable. It can frequently change when individuals become susceptible to vulnerability that causes them to become less shameful and guilty of failure. However, for these individuals, signs of weakness are almost never shown, and instead, they act out their shame and guilt in ultimatums, manipulations, reprisals, and/or suicidal threats.

Narcissism is often characterized by an excessive grandiose ideation of the self, a king who sits at the center of the universe, and all people and things around this "king" shall worship his every need.

Individuals with Narcissistic Personality Disorder (NPD) have extremely fragile self-esteem, and as a way to compensate, they overly enhance their egos and praise toward themselves, refusing to show empathy or weakness to anyone for fear of others discovering their "flaws."

Instead, their delusions drive them to exude a sense of undeserved entitlement, expressing illogical control and emotional manipulation toward those around them.

Individuals suffering from Narcissistic Personality Disorder exhibit similar symptoms to those suffering from Borderline Personality Disorder.

Both personality disorders experience intense fears of abandonment and become unable and unwilling to face the consequences, and instead, twist and downplay the words of their counterparts, constantly feign being the victims, and blame others for all the misfortunes occurring in the narcissists' lives, never accepting defeat or responsibility for their actions.

However, unlike borderliners, narcissists are less likely to engage in self-injurious behaviors as a means of seeking attention. Narcissists are more likely to seek out attention and avoid abandonment by denying and avoiding as opposed to begging and pleading, always putting themselves and their best interests first while disregarding the feelings of others.

Symptoms of those with Narcissistic Personality Disorder include an exaggerated sense of self-importance, with a high delusional obsession for achievement, greatness, praise, and entitlement while taking advantage of others who could potentially benefit them.

They often remain self-absorbed, believing they are destined to be something greater than what life has given them, and they constantly seek out opportunities to enhance their "greatness" even if it means leaving the lives they have behind with no concrete goals to chase after, running after justified self-worth with privilege only they believe they have.

While the exact correlation between individuals with NPD and individuals with BPD has not been widely studied, few studies have found a positive co-occurrence between the two, with 16-39% of individuals suffering from BPD also meeting the diagnostic criteria for NPD.

Research has also shown that narcissistic individuals are more treatment-resistant and less likely to improve when their symptoms also overlap with symptoms of borderliners. Individuals who suffer from this comorbidity are less like to eradicate the symptoms of either disorder (19%) than individuals who only suffer from either NPD or BPD (6%).

The comorbidity of NPD and BPD can prove to be deadly in relationships. Both types of individuals tend to exploit their romantic partners in order to achieve what they want, plus, both groups are often paranoid and extremely fearful of loss and abandonment, creating a stressful emotional apocalypse for the partners in these relationships.

There is substantial evidence that shows how the Dark Triad traits of Machiavellianism, Narcissism, and Psychopathy correspond with the Cluster B personality traits of Antisocial Personality Disorder (APD), Narcissistic Personality Disorder (NPD), Borderline Personality Disorder (BPD), and Histrionic Personality Disorder (HPD), in how individuals who score high on the Dark Triad traits equally score high on the Cluster B personality traits, with psychopathy having the strongest correlation due to its high impulsivity characteristic.

Niccolò di Bernardo dei Machiavelli termed the trait "Machiavellianism" as "dispositional patterns to promote self-related goal achievements regardless of boundaries, rationalizations, or fairness." Individuals with this trait often are aware of the patterns and behaviors they are capable of and engage in but disregard the need to spare the feelings of others when reaching toward their goals.

The Ugly Truth
The Dark Side of Borderline Personality Disorder & The Emotional Mind

Similar to narcissists, Machiavellians seek to take what they believe they are entitled to regardless of who they destroy along the way. These malevolent individuals score high on tests of callousness, impulsivity, coercion, aggression, and grandiosity, seeking thrills and successes regardless of who they inflict pain on or annihilate.

A study by Frodi and colleagues in 2001 identified the Dismissive-Avoidant Attachment Style as the most common descriptor of psychopathic criminals. Similarly, a study by Salteris in 2002 concluded how individuals who commit acts of violence are more likely to experience unstable and disturbed attachment styles.

In adults who experience traits of psychopathy, those with factor one traits are more likely to be linked to a hostile attachment style, with low avoidance and low anxiety, while those with factor two traits are more likely to be linked to a fearful attachment style, with strong avoidance and high anxiety, and are often in coexistence with drug abuse and aggression, consistent with individuals experiencing borderline personality traits and insecure narcissism.

Borderline Personality Disorder has been seen in some of the world's deadliest criminals, more so in female criminals than in males. Among them include Aileen Wuornos, an American serial killer and prostitute who confessed to shooting 7 men in Florida within a time span of 12 months, Jeffrey Dahmer, an American serial killer and sex offender who murdered, dismembered, and cannibalized 17 boys and men in Wisconsin and Ohio, and Kristen Gilbert, an American serial killer and former nurse who murdered 4 men in Massachusetts by injecting

The Ugly Truth
The Dark Side of Borderline Personality Disorder & The Emotional Mind

them with large doses of epinephrine to induce cardiac arrest.

Wuornos dealt with a rough and traumatizing childhood that left irrevocable damage on her psyche. In addition to enduring sexual assault from her grandfather, her mother also abandoned her when she was just a young girl, not realizing this truth until she was 11 years old.

Because of this early abuse, Wuornos developed behavioral problems and explosive temper in her early teens, making it difficult for her to maintain stable relationships as her childhood trauma forced her mind to enter primitive and dissociated mindsets, later being diagnosed with Borderline Personality Disorder at the age of 46.

As a child, Jeffrey Dahmer was severely deprived of attention as his mother suffered from constant depression and suicide attempts. He also discovered his homosexuality, but because of his fear in telling his parents and coming out with his sexuality, he, instead, fantasized about dominating men he could not have by any means possible, including murder.

Despite being diagnosed with BPD, Schizotypal Personality Disorder, and Psychosis during his trial, he was still convicted as legally sane and sentenced to 15 terms of life imprisonment in 1992.

On the outside, Kristen Gilbert seemed like any ordinary young woman, intelligent and with a lively personality. However, her borderline personality overtook her very early as she became addicted to attention, constantly wanting more and more for the thrill and security and

The Ugly Truth
The Dark Side of Borderline Personality Disorder & The Emotional Mind

manipulating her romantic partners into giving her what she wanted.

She had a volatile relationship with her husband while continuing to have affairs even after she had kids. During her 15-month sentence for a possible bomb threat, Gilbert attempted suicide, more for the excitement of drawing attention to herself than for death itself, causing medical authorities to diagnose her as borderline.

Victims of Borderline Personality Disorder almost feel as if they are not themselves, constantly moving in between relationships and hobbies, spontaneously jumping from one person or thing to another.

They experience high highs at the beginning of each new experience they encounter, such as new relationships or a new change, but these excitements never last long as BPD individuals often become bored of their stagnant lifestyles, and their impulsivity overtakes them in seeking something new.

Their constant paranoid thoughts pull them away from positive and healthy factors in life as they overthink even the most minute of incidences, struggling to distinguish between reality and imagination.

It's no wonder why Borderline Personality Disorder has one of the highest rates of suicide compared to all other mental illnesses, with over 75% of borderliners attempting suicide at least once in their lifetimes, and approximately 3-10% of borderliners completing suicide, exponentially higher than the average population.

The Chaos

Borderline Chaos

One quiet morning, Steve and Becca went out to a diner for a hot cup of coffee and some waffles. They had been dating for a year and had been living together for 7 months after Becca gave Steve an ultimatum to either move in together or risk having her walk out of the relationship.

Becca never had an intention of leaving, but the fear of Steve potentially sleeping with other women when she wasn't around drove Becca to the point where she felt the need to keep tabs on her boyfriend at all costs, forcing Steve to give into her demands because she seemed "perfect" in every other way, and he did not want to risk losing her.

Moments after they were seated, more and more people began entering the diner on this bright Sunday morning. As the sound of the pans rattling and the noise of the customers chattering increased, Becca's mind started reminiscing, with constant flashbacks of her traumatic moments as a child when her mother threw dishes at her father while they endlessly argued and fought.

Becca's eyes began twitching, her hands began shaking, and she continued to mutter under her breath for several minutes before Steve noticed her unusual behavior. Just hours ago, they were in bed, laughing and holding each other like they were all each other needed.

"What's wrong, honey?" Steve asked, curious and concerned about Becca's reactions toward the noise in the diner.

"Nothing, just nothing," Becca whispered quietly, her eyes failing to meet her partner's.

Uninterested in pressing the issue further, Steve then reminded Becca that his parents' anniversary is approaching, and that he will be gone for several hours later that afternoon to attend their party. Unexpectedly, he was shocked at Becca's response.

The Ugly Truth
The Dark Side of Borderline Personality Disorder & The Emotional Mind

"What?! You're leaving me!? You can't leave me! You're cheating on me! I knew it! I bet there's no party. You just wanted an excuse to break up with me! Fuck you, Steve! I hate you!! You're dead to me!" Becca exploded at him just seconds before getting down on her knees and kissing his brown loafer shoes, begging for forgiveness and pleading for him to not walk away as the entire diner stared at them.

From an outsider's perspective, Becca's sudden public outburst seemed chaotic, uncalled for, and downright abnormal and psychotic. However, for the 14 million people in the United States alone who are also suffering from Borderline Personality Disorder, her verbal and behavioral outbursts seem like any ordinary day.

Borderliners make up 2% of the general population, but over 20% of the population residing in psychiatric hospitals with women more commonly affected than men. Their unusual rollercoaster of emotions alienates them from the people around them who become ashamed and embarrassed for the association as they often respond to simple situations with explosive outbursts.

If we look at the word "borderline" in Borderline Personality Disorder, the word implies that someone is constantly on the edge, living a risky and impulsive life and never able to stabilize and stand their ground. Their mindsets become a tilting ship, tipping off the edge of a waterfall, unsure of whether to release or remain.

Like most mental illnesses, BPD is a disorder that is not well understood by those who have never experienced it. Borderliners often describe their disease as intense

The Ugly Truth
The Dark Side of Borderline Personality Disorder & The Emotional Mind

adrenaline rushes through their bodies that unconsciously make them act out in ways that go against their moral and logical beliefs to the point where they simply want to curl up in a corner and forget the actions they had done. One moment, they'll apply for law school, and the next, they'll dye their hair pink and become a groupie for a rock band, never truly being able to make up their minds.

Borderliners often jump to conclusions without taking a second to think through the consequences, and they become quick to assume that others have rejected and abandoned them even if it's all in their minds.

Despite the nonexistent evidence, borderliners are stubborn in standing by their perceived viewpoints, feeling hurt and betrayed when they believe others are walking out on them, even if they are just going into a different room, becoming fatally depressed and self-destructive when people leave them even for just a few hours, and becoming suicidal and psychotic when people do not pick up their phone calls on the first ring.

Surprisingly, borderliners are more comfortable during chaotic and stressful moments in relationships than in calm and stable situations because they know how to function in disarray. When relationships are stable, they become overly anxious and unsure of when their partners will leave them, often unprepared for the violence and disturbance that could potentially arise from the stillness before the storm.

On the other hand, when borderliners are amidst in chaos, their assumptions all come true, allowing them to confirm the fears they had since the beginning of the

The Ugly Truth
The Dark Side of Borderline Personality Disorder & The Emotional Mind

relationship. They are used to emotional turmoil as they thrive on manipulating situations from playing out the way they're supposed to and feeling like they are in control even when they are not.

They continue to persist the deterioration of romantic relationships until they have solidified that their initial beliefs were correct, refusing to stop until they have worn the other person down.

According to Otto Kernberg, one of the first psychiatrists to define the borderline personality, BPD arises from the direct experience of physical and/or emotional violence by those around them, paired with biological abnormalities that cause the minds of borderliners to divide into "positive and negative buckets" where they separate positive experiences to avoid them becoming contaminated by the negative ones, such as individuals holding onto the positive memories of their partners despite their partners abusing and abandoning them.

Studies have found exceptionally heightened activity in the amygdala, a brain structure that forms part of the limbic system and regulates both memory and sense of emotional reactiveness, where the reactivity generates a hair-trigger temperature.

Furthermore, several borderline patients have a common short serotonin transporter variant, or 5-HTT gene. It affects the amount of neurotransmitters accessible to nerve cells, and the short allele has been associated with nervous, aggressive, and impulsive conduct.

The Ugly Truth
The Dark Side of Borderline Personality Disorder & The Emotional Mind

Borderliners have a warped perception of time when it comes to dealing with traumatic events and uncertainties, seeing life and the events in them as chapters rather than as a chronological sequence of events where one moment drastically affects the sequential moments that succeed it.

The Ugly Truth
The Dark Side of Borderline Personality Disorder & The Emotional Mind

Part Two

The Ugly Truth
The Dark Side of Borderline Personality Disorder & The Emotional Mind

Controlled by Emotions

Human Beings are Controlled by Their Emotions

We are all controlled by our emotions. Human beings behave in different, and sometimes complex, manners because we frequently allow our emotions to drive our behaviors and influence the decisions we make that concern our lives.

The Ugly Truth
The Dark Side of Borderline Personality Disorder & The Emotional Mind

The external stimuli that we encounter on a day-to-day basis stimulate our internal senses, releasing neurotransmitters that create the emotions that travel with each experiencing thought. This is why we experience similar emotions when similar situations to those of our past's occur as our emotions are tied to the way we process our thoughts.

Human emotions drive our decision-making more than logic and common sense. It is difficult for people to objectively make conscious decisions without allowing their feelings to impact them. The decisions we make when we feel angry versus when we feel sad versus when we feel happy will always be different regardless of whether the situations are the same.

Our emotions drive over 80% of our day to day lives while rationality only influences 20%. Therefore, most of us experience moments where we feel like we have messed up and failed, or where we experience regret because we feel like we made the wrong decisions. This is because we allow our emotions to get inside our heads and control the actions we would have made differently under different circumstances.

Our emotions also cause us to favor our bias toward decisions based on feelings of safety, security, and comfort rather than based on cognitive thinking. Have you ever found yourself thinking, "This doesn't feel right," which in turn, deters you from making a certain decision?

We go against making decisions we don't feel right about despite whether it's the best decision for us because when

The Ugly Truth
The Dark Side of Borderline Personality Disorder & The Emotional Mind

we encounter familiar situations that have turned us off before, our emotions trigger our memories and prevent us from experiencing the same "bad feeling" we had experienced in the past. Our brains are designed to make us feel safe so we avoid repeating an act or being in a situation that has made us feel "bad" in the past despite all the facts and logic supporting it otherwise.

Different emotions affect our decisions in various ways. When we feel dejected, we are more inclined to settle for decisions that go against our favor due to a of lack of motivation and drive to think logically through the consequences.

Emotions are the strong drivers of decision-making because they provide information about our circumstances in the quickest and simplest ways that do not require cognitive skills. We view our emotions as our "default brain" because we tend to trust our instincts more than we trust our knowledge.

Research has shown that the human brain comprises of two parts: the logical part and the emotional part. The logical part of the brain is slow, rational, and allows us to think objectively. This part of the brain lets us deliberate methodically through a list of pros and cons before coming to a conclusion about any given decision.

On the flip side, the emotional part of the brain is more impulsive and instinctive. It drives us to perform actions and behaviors that we are not always aware of performing, creating unconscious awareness in most of our decision-making.

The Ugly Truth
The Dark Side of Borderline Personality Disorder & The Emotional Mind

In fact, most of our emotional lives are lived unconsciously. Because our emotional mind has more influence on our subconscious, as opposed to our logical, mind, it drives our current behaviors to fit a pattern that we already had experience with and trust, and we are more likely to act upon imprints on our subconscious minds rather than reflect and reason with our rational selves.

Humans falsely believe that they abide their lives based on thoughts and decisions controlled by the logical brain, allowing us to feel more enabled and powerful. Truth is, our emotional brains are what really control our lives.

Think about it, we enact decisions based on our thoughts, but our thoughts are often driven by how we feel rather than what we know because our thoughts are often associated with memories and what we know we do or do not like based on past experiences.

For example, people who have experienced trauma in their pasts change their decisions and behaviors based on their thoughts of these past traumatic memories and the adverse feelings they have felt as a result of them as opposed to their current knowledge about said situations.

All the knowledge in the world cannot protect us unless we understand and have lived the experiences of what we can potentially expect.

Emotional intelligence, or our ability to understand, evaluate, and manage the emotions we experience, has been shown to play a more vital role in decision-making than our brains.

The Ugly Truth
The Dark Side of Borderline Personality Disorder & The Emotional Mind

Researchers have found that people suffering brain damage, who have lost their ability to experience emotions, often experience a decreased ability in making beneficial decisions as they have not dealt with the painful feelings that are often paired with poor decision-making.

Our emotions can also influence our attitudes and judgments, which can drastically change the choices we make. Intense sadness can either prevent the self from taking initiative, or it can prevent the self from engaging in impulsive decisions.

Fear of rejection can either prevent the self from stepping outside the comfort zones, or it can prevent the self from contacting potential pain. Despite this, our success largely depends on our ability to understand and interpret how we feel before making quick judgments.

Emotional Prisoners

We are Prisoners of Our Own Emotions

We all have an unlimited amount of emotions that travel within our thoughts. However, sometimes the thoughts that course through our minds are not always for our own benefits and can sometimes even harm us.

Despite what we think we know about fleeting and ever-changing emotions, we still follow the "gut instincts" that go against our well-beings, and we become imprisoned to them. We continue to let our minds construct thoughts and mindsets that disturb our inner peace.

We are prisoners of our own thoughts, whether these thoughts are positive or negative. When these thoughts are positive, they align with our general beliefs that following our "gut instincts" lead to positive results. But when these thoughts are negative and sometimes even distracting, vague, or confusing, we listen to them anyway because we still believe our "gut instincts" know best even as they lead us to our demise. This creates a vicious cycle of dysfunctional behaviors due to destructive thoughts that we continuously try to talk ourselves into by falsely believing that "this time will be different."

Human thoughts come from past conditioning. Our minds and our brains are made up of different components. Our minds are made up of our environmental surroundings, the thoughts that come and go, as well as how much we absorb these thoughts whereas our brains are created based on our genetic makeup.

The thoughts that we experience daily are due to "conditioning." If we carefully dissect and observe our thoughts, we realize that this "noise" is actually comments, explanations, judgments, projections, fantasies, and dreams coming from our minds, all of which are based completely on our own "unique" conditioning.

There is also no such thing as "original thought." The ideas and beliefs that we have acquired and learned growing up act as a base on which newly-conditioned thoughts are added daily and subconsciously.

This is why overthinking situations never actually solve any of our problems. It only serves to give us the illusion that our problems are being resolved and that we are actively working through our issues when in actuality, it serves no purpose. We will always act based on our past conditioning over our current and learned knowledge because experiences are far more powerful.

There is a substantial difference between what we think and what happens in reality. We are all trapped in our own perceptions, which become the only way we interact with the world because that is the only way we can see it.

We are also imprisoned by the circumstances and environment around us, including our bodies, our parents, our cultures, our geography, our technology, our economy, our politics, our influences, our education, and our interactions.

While our memories and our experiences help us maintain a sense of continuity in life, they also hold us captive as we use them to build walls that surround us, imprisoning our open-mindedness and forcing us to see life only through a small-tinted window.

We can never truly experience reality for what it is. Instead, we perceive reality through memories from past experiences and worries about future experiences, creating a distorted version of the present tense. Eventually, we end up living in a cell that defines how we

The Ugly Truth
The Dark Side of Borderline Personality Disorder & The Emotional Mind

will feel and how we will react to any given event or circumstance.

If something fits into our perceptions of life, we feel happy and satisfied, and if it does not, we become hostile, anxious, and depressed. Most people live their entire lives in mental prison cells, confined to the dictators that are their own minds. We think that by locking ourselves within the confines of our own core beliefs without the flexibility to branch out, then we are in control of ourselves.

However, the solace that we foolishly believe we have placed ourselves in is actually causing more harm to us as we remain trapped in only what we already know, with no additional knowledge on how to handle situations that we have not already experienced. Because of this, our minds channel all efforts into protecting our survival rather than allowing us to feel truly free and happy.

Buddha once referred to living inside our own minds, where we constantly avoid the unwanted and become attached to the wanted, as living in suffering rather than living in peace, a constant state of conflict between the "I" and life.

We experience brief moments of relaxation and enjoyment, but because of its automatic nature, our minds quickly return to a state known as the "Monkey Mind," jumping back and forth between the past and the future, taking our focus away and distracting us between what's real and what's only a figment of our imaginations. Time after time, we fail to recognize that

The Ugly Truth
The Dark Side of Borderline Personality Disorder & The Emotional Mind

life does not always play out the way we want it to, and that it is meant to have constant ups and downs.

We are all presented with situations that either play out as stepping stones to higher levels of consciousness, or we stumble on them and fall. When we perceive our circumstances as stepping stones, we transcend and associate these situations and situations like them with "goodness" and something we would engage in again.

On the contrary, when we fail to "win" in situations that are presented to us, we associate similar situations with fear, terrified of encountering these situations again as they have destroyed us once before. Living in fear inside our own minds prevents us from exploring and seeking the "Eternal Truth," hindering us from opening our minds and preventing us from accepting that the true meaning of life cannot be discovered through limited logic.

Tortured by Silence

We are Tortured by Our Silence

Have you ever been in a situation where the words and thoughts are inside your mind but struggle to come out when you try to vocalize them?

However, even during this silence, these thoughts are still expressed subconsciously through feelings and emotions, however, often coming into awareness when it is too late. Our emotions allow us to express ourselves in ways

The Ugly Truth
The Dark Side of Borderline Personality Disorder & The Emotional Mind

where we are unable to filter ourselves for fears of shame or embarrassment.

Our sensations allow us to portray the words we wish we could say to others without the fear of judgment. Our emotions help us overcome the phenomenon we experience known as the "Paralytic Effect," where we allow our painful and shameful memories of the past to silence us from using words to express the thoughts we experience, allowing our emotions to help us overcome this mental paralysis.

We are not used to living in a society where silence is acceptable and welcomed. Our society forces us to associate silence with depression, a torture of the mind, whereas being vocal and expressive is often associated with signs of happiness and optimism.

When we experience a failure in being able to express ourselves the ways we want, we become mentally blockaded by our anxieties of not being heard or understood.

We feel trapped in the abyss of our own minds where we feel like no one could possibly help or understand us, where no one can truly see us for who we are while we continue to stay confined in our self-destructive and vicious cycle of feeling like we are not good enough and should just remain silent. This paralysis results in the loss of individuality the more we feed into our silence, and we begin to feel depersonalized and forgotten.

Despite using our emotions over 80% of the time to express how we are, human beings are still, to this day,

The Ugly Truth
The Dark Side of Borderline Personality Disorder & The Emotional Mind

afraid of allowing others to see how they really feel, attempting to push all their reactions down even as they are reaching their breaking points.

Why are we so afraid of expressing simple sensations that everyone also experiences, sensations that can help save our very lives? Some of us have the fear of allowing our emotions to clash with the opinions or emotions of others, wanting to avoid rather than stir up conflict.

Unless it's our own emotions, not a lot of people are mature enough to handle the passions of others without taking it personally or feeling uncomfortable. Therefore, we avoid showing our true feelings to avoid relationship divergences caused by possible dismissals of us if we opt to be honest.

Similar to this, there are those who reject the idea of having emotions at all. To them, emotions are associated with imperfections and flaws, leaving the person feeling defenseless, powerless, and vulnerable for the attack of predators if they let their guards down. They fear that emotions give others reasons to dismiss them as weak and frail if they shed one tear or throw one punch.

Our reservations of being dismissed or disregarded by others if we show even a hint of vulnerability drive us to hide our emotions for life to avoid any types of rejection or disapproval.

We literally set ourselves up for a lifetime of misery and agony just to satisfy our inordinate needs to please those we don't even know and to avoid making them feel miserable and agonized.

The Ugly Truth
The Dark Side of Borderline Personality Disorder & The Emotional Mind

Sometimes, we end up holding in our true feelings for so long that we no longer accept that it is worth expressing anything about ourselves, pulling us into this black abyss where our self-esteem become so low that we are convinced that our lives will never be worth pursuing and that our relationships will never make us happy, leading us down a cycle of hopelessness.

As a result, we begin to accept that our lives remain stagnant and that if we're not happy or satisfied by this point in our lives, then we never will be. However, it's not the truth in the matter that causes us to remain stuck in our patterns of ineptness; it's the constant mindset we possess where we have told ourselves so many times that we are not allowed to express how we feel or what we want that these beliefs turn into reality.

Others, however, repress their emotions for more active than passive reasons of trepidation. They believe they can use their emotions as a way of manipulating the feelings of others into doing what they want, such as using sadness to drive others to pity them or using anger to cause others to fear them.

They sometimes also believe that those close to them, or even not close to them, should automatically know what and how they feel even without them needing to express themselves. This belief that the self is the center of attention rings true for many as they often expect others to simply give them what they want without them needing to ask for it.

Some people also act as martyrs when it comes to emotions, refusing to accept that they have any kinds of

The Ugly Truth
The Dark Side of Borderline Personality Disorder & The Emotional Mind

emotions other than happiness and joy, always trying to please others and refusing to acknowledge self-pain.

They invest wholeheartedly in controlling their feelings so when they experience anger or hatred, they do not know how to react. They often race to avoid as a way of solving their issues rather than dealing with them head on and disclosing their feelings as the fear of judgment and criticism is always right around the corner.

It takes a lot of courage and effort for people to be able to express how they feel and to share their opinions. Doing so puts them in vulnerable positions where they will either thrive or perish, and it's that anxiety, that unknown, that keeps people from wanting to self-express, weighing the costs over the benefits, and ultimately bottling up their feelings inside.

Normopathy

Emotions are the Key Drivers of Normopathy

Christopher Bollas once described normopathy as the "state of being obsessed with fitting in with society, to the point where individuals completely lose their personalities."

Normopaths often pursue to conform to the beings and lifestyles of others in attempts to gain society's approval at the expense of their basic need to express their own individualities, their survivals depending more on social approval and validation than on self-approval and authentication.

This constant preoccupation with trying to be "normal" and blend in with everyone else is often used as a defense mechanism in attempts to hide behaviors that normopaths believe others will condemn, thus, causing them to become extremely self-conscious, intensely focusing on how they appear to others and the constant need to impress them.

Unfortunately, normopathy is a socially-accepted reality that represents our collective and neurotic denial of our true selves to protect our bodies and our minds from emotional injuries.

Although it isn't necessarily a flaw or a danger to ourselves to develop this belief of being like everyone else, it only becomes a problem when our neurotic thoughts cause anxiety and anger that begin to interfere with our daily functioning.

Normopaths can become so out of touch with reality that they begin to live in an imaginary world where their pursuits to "fit in" and "belong" impair their personal performance, personal identification, individual well-being, personal success, and ultimately, their entire beings.

But what causes seemingly normal individuals to become normopaths? What causes someone to have such a strong desire to fit in that they willingly throw themselves away? Normopaths are usually sprouted during childhood, where children have tried to express their voices just to

The Ugly Truth
The Dark Side of Borderline Personality Disorder & The Emotional Mind

be shot down time after time or have tried to dress in a way that they preferred just to be teased and ridiculed, causing them to associate "having opinions" and "being different" with "hatred" and "isolation."

They soon develop this core belief that they must blend in with the rest of society in order to avoid more hatred and isolation even at the expense of completely losing themselves, leaving them vulnerable to others and blindly following misrepresented words even if they do not agree.

Thus, normopaths are left feeling crippled and paralyzed, unable to speak or think unless given permission to do so, and they develop intense social anxiety, avoiding new situations and even new people for the fear of further mockery.

Another disadvantage for normopaths is that individuals who suffer from normopathy often become acutely aware of those who do act out of the norm and outside of the constant patterns. Seeing someone in an outrageous outfit or hearing someone speak against the "rules" triggers a reaction in normopaths that can range from discomfort to rage to disgust.

They speak out erratically and spontaneously when they see others going against societal standards in attempts to relieve themselves from their own discomforts, sometimes even at the cost of their careers or relationships.

When we spend decades and decades hiding our true emotions, we end up wearing our masks permanently to hide our secrets and protect our fragile egos from the pain of rejection.

The Ugly Truth
The Dark Side of Borderline Personality Disorder & The Emotional Mind

We eventually become psychologically dead and emotionally drained, unable to feel our own emotions and constantly taking on the emotions of those around us. We flee from potential emotional terror and into the arms of social conformity and self-destruction as we shut ourselves off from the pain of lost and betrayal, living an inauthentic life on the face of the Earth like an imprint of another individual trying to achieve perfectionism and giving up ourselves.

But who's to say what's right or wrong? Who's to say which are the correct "rules" we follow? The ones who hold the most power are always the ones who hold the most confidence and refuse to bow down to the injustice of others.

Normopaths become who they are because their insecurities cause them to doubt their own judgments and beliefs, and they resort to obeying the judgments and beliefs of others because they think they're "better."

Human beings want to fit in so much that they lose their sense of self-worth by engaging in actions they don't even enjoy just to avoid feeling like outcasts. We give up on acknowledging our greatness, and we refuse to overachieve because then, we would be seen as "different" and "weird."

We are so desperate to please others and become what's considered "normal" that we dissociate ourselves from our inner beings, leaving us in a pathological, borderline, and eventual diabolical state.

The Ugly Truth
The Dark Side of Borderline Personality Disorder & The Emotional Mind

When we no longer recognize who we are or what we want, what happens when we can no longer hold in our raging instinctual emotions? What happens when we finally feel like we have to express ourselves or risk mental explosion?

We become volatile and unstable, going back and forth between extreme and impulsive decisions because we are unsure of the goals we aim for as we become lost and forgotten in a world that only strives to promote the goodness of themselves.

Incapable of Sympathy

Human Beings are Incapable of True Sympathy

Contrary to empathy, where we pretend to put ourselves in the shoes of others to understand their woes and sorrows, sympathy is a directed feeling of care and concern toward others with the desire for their well-beings and happiness. Sympathy usually implies a sense of shared similarities with others, promoting personal engagement.

The Ugly Truth
The Dark Side of Borderline Personality Disorder & The Emotional Mind

However, unlike empathy, sympathy does not imply shared perspective or shared emotions as sympathizing with someone is not the same as feeling concern for someone.

When we sympathize, we fool ourselves into believing that we are internalizing the feelings and emotions of others, understanding them. However, we can never truly feel sympathy toward someone else's pain because, in truth, we don't actually care about others, how they're feeling, or what they're going through.

We pretend to sympathize with others because we have been taught to care about others when in reality, we are self-absorbed, only listening enough to relieve ourselves from our guilt and never truly understanding the pain of others.

However, we are also unable to truly sympathize with others because of our own emotional blocks such as anger and envy.

When someone close to us is in agony, rather than getting our heads out of our asses to help them, we remain stuck in our closed mindsets, feeling anger toward the person for not listening to us in the first place or for committing acts we believe are stupid and idiotic, and instead of being there for the victim, we become disdained and detached from the present tense, unable to feel sorrow for someone who we believe behaved foolishly.

We also become detached from being able to express true sympathy because sometimes the pain of others forces us to reminisce about our own pain, the very same pain we

The Ugly Truth
The Dark Side of Borderline Personality Disorder & The Emotional Mind

have spent years avoiding and creating an emotional barrier toward.

We become selfish, and we perceive the victim as a trigger for our own emotional agony rather than as an innocent individual who needs our help. Because of this, we do everything we can to protect ourselves, acting in ways we wouldn't otherwise because we feel the need to prevent ourselves from pain at all costs, even if it means losing relationships because we cannot stand the suffering of others.

We find it easier to abandon and ghost people than be there for them in their time of need. This often happens when we are unable to separate emotions from personal pasts, absorbing the feelings of others as our own rather than seeing them as something external to us.

Like empathy, sympathy is an innate and learned skill that is often affected by how our environments and lifestyles have shaped us. In order to experience these skills, we would have had to have been taught how to separate our pain from the pain of others and be open and honest with ourselves enough to avoid triggering repressed feelings when we experience the feelings of others.

We lack these skills because, for so long, we have been condemned for having feelings and taught to shut them down whenever they arise at all costs, making us incapable of relating to or experiencing the feelings of others without taking offense.

The Ugly Truth
The Dark Side of Borderline Personality Disorder & The Emotional Mind

As a result of not being able to portray compassion toward others, we end up lacking compassion toward ourselves, leaving us disconnected from our authentic selves and incapable of sympathizing with ourselves when we truly need it.

We use this disconnection with ourselves and others as a form of defense mechanism for our egos because we feel that if we sympathize, we open ourselves to the potential of taking in the pain of others, and many of us have tried to avoid pain for so long that we are not mentally prepared to even come into contact with the pain of others.

Because of this disconnection and fear of vulnerability, we resort to reacting selfishly with zero concern for the sensations of others, focusing more on status and benefit toward ourselves that we would rather lose others than attempt to understand them.

We have the tendency to behave selfishly, only looking out for what's best for us, that we lose the ability to hesitate when it comes to banishing the needs of others.

Don't get me wrong, it's not like human beings are completely incapable of sympathizing with others; it is in our inherent natures to want to help those around us. However, for so long, we have trained our brains to not care that apathy becomes almost instinctual as if we don't even notice when we dismiss others.

The Ugly Truth
The Dark Side of Borderline Personality Disorder & The Emotional Mind

Humans are Impulsive

We React Toward Life Situations Based on Impulsivity and Fleeting Feelings

Most of us believe that the way we behave is based on pure logic and common sense. However, what we continue to live in denial about is that our behaviors are often driven by our raw emotions rather than our intellects.

The Ugly Truth
The Dark Side of Borderline Personality Disorder & The Emotional Mind

This goes back to how we find it difficult to separate our logical selves from our emotional selves, actively pushing aside our emotional brains to prevent them from overpowering our logical brains when it is almost impossible to do so.

We often don't realize what we're doing until we are in the midst of doing it, constantly acting on impulses and sudden shifts in emotion, a dangerous pattern we all face. However, despite how much we realize this is happening, we STILL find difficulty preventing our emotions from taking over; that's because we can't.

Our emotions are a permanent and constant part of us, a subjective state of mind that behaves as a reaction to our internal or external stimuli such as our memories or surroundings.

However, emotions themselves are not always considered "good" or "bad"; they are simply an expression of our reactions to events occurring around us, impacting our decisions toward certain situations at any given time. Our emotions always play a key role in our daily lives despite how much we believe our decisions are based on lucidity and rationality.

The concept of "Emotional Intelligence" is our ability to understand and manage our emotions rather than letting them roam free impulsively and spontaneously. However, managing our emotions differs greatly from suppressing them. When we ignore our feelings, pushing away the pain we are meant to feel, we are neglecting our mind's way of telling us that something is wrong and needs to be dealt with.

The Ugly Truth
The Dark Side of Borderline Personality Disorder & The Emotional Mind

Ignoring our feelings doesn't automatically make the pain go away; it just further pushes down feeling after feeling until the pain becomes so great that we are no longer able to manage the emotions effectively and as a result, we let them run rogue and negatively impact our decision-making, such as turning toward unhealthy coping mechanisms.

In contrast, there are also those who prevent the suppression of their feelings altogether, letting their emotions take charge of their lives at all times, acting impulsively and wildly without keeping their emotions in check and scanning their surroundings to ensure the appropriate situations.

These individuals tend to lack emotional intelligence and instead, behave like animals, living solely off their instincts and acting on temporary emotions rather than recognizing which emotions should be released and which should be quelled.

Temporary emotions include wanting to smash a car out of anger that someone instigated, wanting to eat everything in sight even when on a diet, or wanting to blurt hurtful words without considering the feelings of others. Individuals with Borderline Personality Disorder often act out solely based on temporary emotions, which in the long run, can lead to dangerous and fatal consequences.

Because Borderline Personality Disorder is most commonly characterized by impulsive reactions and emotional outbursts toward situations that are out of their control, it's no wonder that BPD victims have a negative correlation with emotional intelligence.

Impulsivity is a characteristic where those experiencing it fail to take the time to reflect on their feelings before acting upon them. They let their emotions run wild despite the situation and costs of the situation. Once borderliners decide they want something or have a temporary goal in mind, their emotions are ready to be unleashed, regardless of who they hurt in doing so.

Many people without personality disorders suppress their emotions, taking in and observing their surrounding situations and circumstances before unleashing the beasts inside their minds. Individuals suffering from BPD, however, fail to possess this ability to quell their overwhelming feelings, causing them to not realize the consequences of their emotions until the damages are too great.

While emotions are seen as a method of self-expression when verbal words have become silenced for most individuals, borderliners view emotions as their entire beings, relying on them wholeheartedly to help them respond to life and to grab hold of what they desire, trusting solely on their natural and raw instincts rather than their common sense.

According to a study by Gardner and colleagues in 2009, 523 adults were measured on four features of Borderline Personality Disorder: affective instability, identity disturbance, negative relationships, and self-harm using the Mayer-Salovey-Caruso Emotional Intelligence Test (MSCEIT) and the Schutte Emotional

The Ugly Truth
The Dark Side of Borderline Personality Disorder & The Emotional Mind

Intelligence Scale (SEIS). As predicted, they found a negative correlation between measures of emotional intelligence and borderline personality traits, especially in the ability to manage emotions, confirming the emotional dysregulation of this disorder.

Willpower often refers to how our minds are able to handle the influx of emotions our bodies experience, and the efforts we make in attempts to control our impulsive behaviors when they arise.

There are three components to every emotion: the subjective, the physiological, and the expressive. The subjective component refers to how an individual experiences a given emotion caused by a given situation. Some individuals are more prone to certain types of emotions, like anger or sadness, than others, some of whom experience indifference toward situations that would normally negatively impact others.

The physiological component refers to how an individual's body reacts to said emotion, such as the feeling of tensing up or experiencing heart palpitations. Finally, the expressive component refers to how an individual behaves in response to the emotion being experienced, either choosing to act upon it and create havoc on those around, suppress it and create fatal consequences on their own mind, or dissect it and figure out why they are experiencing the feeling and how to rationally handle it in a healthy manner.

The Ugly Truth
The Dark Side of Borderline Personality Disorder & The Emotional Mind

Those who tend to behave more impulsively in response to their emotions are often those who have been drained of their emotional strengths and willpower to deal with the constant arising situations, giving into their urges and desires because self-control has been too difficult and painful.

There are several factors that can lead to a depletion of emotional strength, including ego depletion and cognitive load. Ego depletion refers to constantly having to deal with situations where the mind conflicts with the emotions, a constant battle between wanting and not being able to have, trying but grasping onto the last straw in attempts to succeed.

This constant back and forth ultimately leads to a loss of motivation and determination, causing individuals to give into their urges as a way to end the war.

Cognitive load, such as having to deal with overwhelming stress, is often a gateway for people to behave impulsively, dealing with so many emotions and situations at once that they run out of space in their logical thinking to react rationally to the uprising emotion, forgetting how to react other than with instinctual impulse because their convoluted minds no longer have space to store the influx of feelings.

The Ugly Truth
The Dark Side of Borderline Personality Disorder & The Emotional Mind

Struggle to See Beyond

We Struggle to See Beyond Our Current Emotions and Life Circumstances

The human mind knows no limit. Some say the mind is a sanctuary, a heavenly place where we can imagine ourselves and let ourselves grow and develop into beautiful and strong individuals.

The Ugly Truth
The Dark Side of Borderline Personality Disorder & The Emotional Mind

Others, however, perceive the human mind as a burning fire of hell, closed doors where we trap ourselves behind when we are ready to relinquish and die. Although neither perception is completely right, all of us have experienced both ideals at one point or another in our lives.

Most of us understand the struggle and grit it takes to feel like we're literally walking from one of those places to the other, the agony we all strive to avoid by preventing our minds from wandering altogether.

However, what we don't realize is that many of us are already living behind closed doors in the burning fires of hell, living comfortably in it as we become blind-sighted by how our refusals to express ourselves means that we are already mentally near death. We become blinded by the smoke that arises from our burning emotions struggling to escape, clouding our perceptions and inflicting pain upon ourselves when we are unsure as to why.

Eventually, we give up on trying to keep this fog from overpowering us that, rather than accepting that this smoke is just our emotions trying to roam free, we drive ourselves crazy trying to continue to push this smoke aside, seeing no way out, and turning to suicide as the ultimate way out of our miseries.

However, we have only come to this point because society has told us that expressing our emotions, especially the negative ones, can wreak havoc on us and cause the world to lock us in isolation for being outcasts. We live in a world where sharing our true feelings with each other warrant criticisms and laughter, forcing us to literally lock ourselves away or suppress our emotions from public eyes.

Because of this, some of us would rather remain stuck in the hell inside our minds, securely holding onto the emotions and refusing to let them loose, than live freely in a place where our minds are no longer convoluted.

We all crave to be individuals, but at the same time, we loathe ourselves for not being able to fit in with the standards of others, causing us to remain stuck in a cage where we constantly crave something we cannot have.

Suicidal thoughts are not uncommon when we remain stuck in our own minds with the refusal to accept that our emotions are not meant to be held inside under lock and key. These thoughts often strike when we feel hopeless that our situations will ever change, when we feel like we no longer have control over our lives and begin to lose meaning and purpose, or when we feel like we must bow down to the biased rules of others in order to stay alive in this messed up modern world.

We experience suicidal thoughts when we feel like we have fought the fight but end up losing every single time, struggling to hold something together as it breaks apart in our palms.

However, we only remain trapped in this suicidal mindset because we allow ourselves to be. By locking our emotions inside our heads, we're basically giving victory to those around us who may or may not even know what

The Ugly Truth
The Dark Side of Borderline Personality Disorder & The Emotional Mind

they're talking about and allowing them to cause obliteration to ourselves.

We are the only ones who can put ourselves in danger's way, just like we are the only ones who can take ourselves out of our suicidal miseries and see that we are the only ones forcing ourselves to live in a world we do not want.

We are trapped and encased by how we are taught to see the world, seeing our lives as a reflection of the lives of society and incapable of perceiving ourselves beyond the delinquents and degenerates we have falsely convinced ourselves to be.

Objectively Impossible

Thinking Objectively is Almost Impossible

Many of us foolishly believe that we are truly capable of thinking and perceiving the world in an objective manner, where we are able to take all the components of a situation and piece them together without allowing our own biases to get in the way. False.

The Ugly Truth
The Dark Side of Borderline Personality Disorder & The Emotional Mind

We, as human beings, are only able to perceive the world subjectively, where we always, subconsciously or not, allow our biased views and opinions to affect the way we perceive any given situation.

For example, if we perceive a fight between a man and a woman in the middle of the street, depending on our preconceived notion about the male and female genders, we will automatically and biasedly choose one side over the other, claiming "facts" such as "he must have instigated the argument first" or "she probably deserved it" without fully understanding the entire story.

No one is able to perceive a situation 100% objectively as we have opinions of our own that will always entice our favorability toward one side or the other.

When we observe situations, we will always observe them based on our past experiences because we don't know any other way. We also cannot truly fact check the reality of given situations because even if we question the perpetrators at the scene of the crime, their subjective answers will in turn skew our subjective beliefs, never truly knowing which to accept as truth.

Even if we try to view a situation as independent of ourselves, there will always be a gap between how a situation appears on the outside and what's really going on in the situation behind the scene.

For example, take the man and the woman arguing. On the outside, it may look like a couple quarreling due to some sort of disagreement or domestic instability. However, for all we know, that "couple" could just be

The Ugly Truth
The Dark Side of Borderline Personality Disorder & The Emotional Mind

strangers who were in some kind of accident moments before or friends exclaiming in loud tones that come off as disputes.

We tend to focus our beliefs and judgments based solely on what we "see," never truly getting down to the points that transcend external appearances, never being able to make a conclusion based on the ENTIRE story, and therefore, making it difficult for us to truly perceive any given situation objectively.

The Ugly Truth
The Dark Side of Borderline Personality Disorder & The Emotional Mind

Stuck Inside Mind

We Remain Stuck Inside our Own Minds, Creating a Myriad of Internal Problems and Complications

Our brains are incredible and ever-functioning organs that constantly work their gears to ensure our survivals. They make it almost impossible to truly stop thinking because our brains like to acknowledge and assess all circumstances and scenarios that are occurring around us even when we are not facing a conflict.

The Ugly Truth
The Dark Side of Borderline Personality Disorder & The Emotional Mind

Have you ever tried to sit down to meditate, only to find your mind wandering and distracted less than a minute later? Our brains are regularly moving, sometimes even to our demise. This happens when we often overthink. Overthinking an external situation or an internal flaw can become detrimental when we focus our brains on these negative circumstances.

Our brains do not understand how to filter good situations from bad so when we overthink how flawed our appearances are, our brains become obsessive in those thoughts, eventually spiraling into low self-esteem of not being good enough and feeling a lack of self-love due to feeling unloved by others.

Our brains are designed to worry, always seeking the next big thing to "fix" or "update." This component, although can create failure to our self-esteem, can help us create the greatest of creations by allowing us the chance at imagination.

Our minds weren't built to keep us optimistic and blissful all the time. We aren't meant to be upbeat and positive individuals; our brains were created to allow us to feel content in any given situation by allowing us to solve the problems around us to live stable lives.

However, when we overthink, our perceptions become occluded where we are only able to see the world from one perspective, such as the one perspective of not feeling good enough, not being valued enough, or not feeling loved enough, where our brains begin to convince us that these self-generated thoughts are truths, creating a lifetime of traumatic and psychological complications.

The Ugly Truth
The Dark Side of Borderline Personality Disorder & The Emotional Mind

When we train our brains to focus on one aspect of our thoughts, they do, turning toward unnecessary and toxic thoughts and away from productive and efficient mindsets that we need to possess to survive in this world. Fortunately, our brains also possess a skill known as "Neuroplasticity," where they have the capacity to change patterns of thinking over the course of a person's lifetime depending on which direction they are being directed toward.

Human beings love living inside their own heads, where the thoughts and surroundings are familiar, safe, and comfortable. This way, we can avoid stressing over the anxieties of "what if" and fearing for the potential unknown despite whether our current mindsets are self-destructive because living in discomfort triumphs living in fear.

We find comfort in staying in our problems because we know what to expect. Our familiar enigmas make us feel like we're beating life because no one is meant to go through life without experiencing some sort of problem or issue. When we live in tension and mayhem, that is, when we feel like we are alive, we are only alive in anguish. This has been especially true over the last decade or so, where social media has idealized struggles and depressing thoughts as the "norm," to the point where if we don't experience depressive thoughts, then we are not living life "well-enough."

The social media world has caused us to become trapped inside our own emotions because an indication of emotional expression is usually met with criticism and hate from Internet trolls. The sole purpose of Internet trolls is to demote our self-esteem as they find value in bringing others down.

Internet platforms such as Facebook and Instagram drown their users with subliminal messages that cause them to go against themselves and their true values. Authentic posts on Instagram about true happiness or true sadness are often met with hateful comments telling users to go kill themselves because they're "too fat to deserve happiness" or they "should just die instead of posting about their misery."

Because of this constant negativity, social media platform users have turned away from posting about their true feelings, and instead, turn to monotonous emotions and boastful bragging of materialistic things and accomplishments because they can still gain all the attention and fame without all the crushing emotional pain.

Thus, we find ourselves imprisoned inside our own gruesome emotions, emotions that continue to pile on top of each other, and we lock ourselves in beneath them as we have lost our outlet to escape from our own minds. Because we have lost this escape toward freedom, we eventually become mind-fucked and explode when we find that we are no longer able to hold in our volatile feelings of anguish.

The human mind is designed to constantly evolve and survive not just to get by on chance or live based on the ideals of others. When we suffer, it is because we have given up on trying to achieve greatness not because we are finally living life.

The Ugly Truth
The Dark Side of Borderline Personality Disorder & The Emotional Mind

Suffering and depressive thoughts cause us to remain stuck in the past, incessantly ruminating on events that had already happened instead of focusing on changing current events, causing us to remain stuck in our preconceived philosophies. This inevitably causes us to live in monotony, accepting defeat and torment as the norm rather than the exception.

We end up becoming powerless in our own lives, enduring endless distress as everyday life. Circumstances around us are neither good nor bad, neither destructive nor prominent; it's our reactions to them and how we choose to connect with those circumstances that dictate how our lives will turn out.

When we choose to give our powers away to our surroundings, we are actively choosing to give our lives away to those we don't even know. When we hold our emotions in and shelter them from the world, we are telling everyone around us that our lives matter that much less than theirs.

The Ugly Truth
The Dark Side of Borderline Personality Disorder & The Emotional Mind

The Ugly Truth
The Dark Side of Borderline Personality Disorder & The Emotional Mind

The Ugly Truth
The Dark Side of Borderline Personality Disorder & The Emotional Mind

www.ingramcontent.com/pod-product-compliance
Lightning Source LLC
Chambersburg PA
CBHW031157020426
42333CB00013B/713